Toward Humanistic Education

TOWARD HUMANISTIC EDUCATION

A Curriculum of Affect

Edited by
Gerald Weinstein and Mario D. Fantini

Foreword by Edward J. Meade, Jr.

Published for the Ford Foundation by

PRAEGER PUBLISHERS
New York · Washington · London

PRAEGER PUBLISHERS
111 Fourth Avenue, New York, N.Y. 10003, U.S.A.
5, Cromwell Place, London S.W.7, England

Published in the United States of America in 1970
by Praeger Publishers, Inc.

Second printing, 1971

To our wives, Kit Weinstein and Temmy Fantini

CONTENTS

FOREWORD

EDWARD J. MEADE, JR.

D espite the apparent (and often real) sluggishness with which schools and colleges respond to new conditions, educational programs and institutions are constantly changing. Education takes the world as its subject; it is the process by which we learn of the past and the present in order to shape the future. At the same time, of course, education acts on the world of which it is a part; educational processes and programs are instruments for changing the world. Taken alone, either one of these missions—understanding the world and altering it—is difficult enough; together, they are enormously more difficult and sometimes even in conflict. In America, this dual mission is further complicated by the responsibility of educational institutions to teach an infinite variety of human beings, differing in interests, abilities, and experiences.

Today the complex dynamics of education are undergoing examination on an unprecedented scale. Not only educational researchers and psychologists specializing in learning behavior but also political scientists, economists, sociologists, and other social scientists (to say nothing of journalists, government officials, parents, and students themselves) are scrutinizing all facets of education. A good deal of this work has been stimulated by private foundations. In the 1960's they were joined in force by the federal government.

The Fund for the Advancement of Education * and its parent body, the Ford Foundation, have supported educational research and experimentation largely through the traditional pattern of philanthropy—granting funds to other organizations and individuals; rarely have they staffed a project of their own. One of the exceptions to this pattern is the subject of this report. In the mid-1960's, no single agency had proposed a fundamental approach and materials that seemed to be relevant and effective for teaching youngsters from poor, minority-group families in the general public schools. The Fund itself undertook an action-research effort known as the Elementary School Teaching Project (ESTP). (The social context of the project—the historical nature of American school curricula, the wave of curriculum reform following Sputnik, the increasing concern with the disadvantaged—is sketched in Chapter I.)

As director of ESTP, the Fund engaged Mario D. Fantini, who, as Director of the Madison School Project, had been working to develop improved programs of instruction in a

* The Fund for the Advancement of Education was established by the Ford Foundation in 1951 to encourage, stimulate, and assist efforts to improve education. The Fund and the Foundation began coordinating their activities in 1957, at which time the staff of the Fund and the Foundation's education division became one and the same. In April 1967, the Fund announced that it would conclude its program as a separate organization and that its general purposes and activities would henceforth be carried forward by the Foundation.

group of public schools in a ghetto neighborhood of Syracuse, New York. During the first year of ESTP, Mr. Fantini was assisted by Miss Lila Phillips, then a staff member of *The Grade Teacher* and now on the staff of the Center for Urban Education, in New York City.

In 1965, Mr. Fantini joined the Ford Foundation staff in Public Education, and Gerald Weinstein, now at the University of Massachusetts School of Education, became director of ESTP. Assisting Mr. Weinstein in 1965–67 were Miss Suzanne Thatcher, now with the Washington, D.C., office of the Education Development Center, and Mrs. Diane Bertine, a writer-editor. The project staff had the help of many others —researchers, teachers, scholars, administrators, and pupils.

As the study progressed, it became evident that the problem of curricula of insufficient interest or relevance was not limited to low-income, black children or to the elementary grades. A growing number of educators were in substantial agreement that cognitively oriented materials and lessons alone were inadequate for many pupils. Rather than work toward more relevant materials in the cognitive domain—the realm of the intellect—the staff therefore took another direction, concentrating its explorations in the realm of affect, the realm of emotion and feeling.

This report presents the results of these explorations over two and a half years. The search included designing, field testing, reviewing, and analyzing curricula . . . and agonizing. The members of the project staff and we of the Fund and Foundation freely acknowledge that its contents are neither definitive nor complete. But it does represent a start in the direction of a curriculum alternative based on the affective characteristics of all children—characteristics that transcend variations in economic and social background and that may be relevant to the very core of what makes all children want to learn and grow.

We offer this report in the hope that it will stimulate further inquiry and work on the role of affective behavior in determining the substance and process of education in the early years of school.

Participants in the Elementary School Teaching Project

Staff:

Mario D. Fantini (Director, 1964–65)
Gerald Weinstein (Director, 1965–67)
Lila J. Phillips (Associate Director, 1964–65)
Diane Bertine (Staff Assistant, 1965–67)
Suzanne Thatcher (Staff Assistant, 1965–67)

Field Staff:

Joseph Bongo	Robert Lesniak
Terry Borton	Emma Plattor
Hope Danielson	Stanton Plattor
Marvin Gerber	Julian Roberts
Martin Haberman	John Tibbetts

Consultants to the Field Staff:

Herbert Otto   Stewart Shapiro   Hall T. Sprague

Toward Humanistic Education

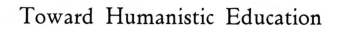

1

INTRODUCTION

The present crisis in the education of poor, minority-group children is holding up a mirror to the educational system as a whole, forcing educators to look more closely at virtually all of their assumptions about learning and teaching. Increasingly, educational theories and practices are being judged on whether they succeed with the urban poor and others who are accounted educational failures. If they do, they will probably be effective with other learners as well. Thus, society as a whole has an immediately practical, as well as ultimately moral, stake in what educators learn about improving the education of those at the bottom of the educational ladder. This book reports the findings of a project originally undertaken in an attempt to discover ways of improving the education of this group—an attempt that led to the formulation of a new approach to the education of *all* children.

The nature of the school curriculum in the United States has long been a focus of inquiry and contention, particularly the curriculum in elementary schools—the content, materials, methods, and goals of teachers working with our nation's younger pupils. In an earlier day, public elementary-school teaching had a strong moral tone. Curriculum was used to indoctrinate youngsters into "the American way of life" as it was defined at that period in history. Later the emphasis was on ways of helping immigrant children to understand their new country. Then the focus shifted again, this time toward understanding one's neighbor and society in general.

More recently, the curriculum has emphasized the preparation of children for learning about the natural and social sciences. Spurred by the race for space, the nation's lawmakers urged educators, scholars, and laymen to develop the "hard curriculum" of the natural sciences, mathematics, and foreign languages. To back up their entreaties, they pushed open the door to federal aid to elementary and secondary education. At the same time, there were cries from an alarmed public that "Johnny can't read" and that the schools, eager to equip the young with social and scientific skills had neglected basic learning tools. These and other pressures produced a stream of subject-matter studies and materials and an alphabet soup of curriculum enterprises—PSSC (Physical Science Study Committee), BCSC (Biological Curriculum Study Commission), CBI (Chemical Bond Instruction), and others.

The results of this intensive curriculum work have been remarkable. The fundamental concepts of some curricula have changed. In many areas, new methodologies—programmed instruction, computer-assisted instruction, tutorials, large- and small-group instruction, and a variety of individualized instruction procedures—have been developed.

But in the late 1950's the nation began to awaken to the fact that thousands of poor, minority-group youngsters in

America's public schools were handicapped not only economically and socially but educationally as well. So-called disadvantaged pupils were not necessarily different from middle-class children in aptitudes or interests, but they differed in the ability to take advantage of the typical American school, whose curriculum was academic, cognitively oriented, and attuned to a middle-class cultural background and whose style and processes were foreign to their environment and experience. Whether these pupils lived in the racial ghettoes of large cities or in the outreaches of America, they were in classrooms ill-suited to their needs.

Educators and academicians have found it difficult to respond effectively to the needs and demands of these youngsters. The challenges they present are not the kinds with which traditional curriculum specialists, much less scholars in universities, are accustomed to working. Although these pupils may possess high levels of intellect, they are mired down by lack of opportunity, years of neglect and indifference, and, often, racial prejudice. For these reasons, the Sputnik-inspired curriculum reform of the 1950's did not meet the needs of such youngsters. Increasingly, educators are realizing that how one goes about teaching is very closely related to what one tries to teach. The poor, minority-group pupil has dramatized the lesson that no teaching procedure can be effecive if the content is of little interest to the class.

Even more fundamental than the question of how and what we teach, however, is the question of *why* we teach what we do. There is little disagreement among educators about one of the broad objectives of teaching in a free society —to help people function constructively as citizens. However, what people have been taught and how they behave are not necessarily consonant. For example, few who have been to school have escaped exposure to the concepts of equality and justice somewhere in the curriculum. Yet the attitudes and actions of many citizens with regard to social injustice suggest that what they have been taught is not affecting their behavior.

With these problems as background, in the late 1950's,

the Ford Foundation and the Fund for the Advancement of Education, which had undertaken various efforts to improve elementary and secondary education, began to concentrate on problems of the low-income, minority-group student. The new emphasis took several paths. The Fund began, and the Foundation expanded, a program of assistance to pilot projects in school improvement in the deprived sections of several large cities.[1] Early experiments in preschool education, precursors of the government-supported Project Headstart, also were supported by grants from the Fund and the Foundation. Multipurpose community-improvement grants in selected cities were intended in part to coordinate the efforts of urban public schools with the work of public and private agencies concerned with the health, welfare, and economic status of the inner-city family.[2] College- and university-based experiments to improve the preparation of teachers generally turned to special training to equip teachers to deal more effectively with the learning problems of the children of poverty. In addition, a variety of action and research projects was supported, ranging from basic studies to child development to studies of the language problems of disadvantaged children.

Finally, in 1964, the Fund undertook an action project of its own, an attempt to develop a curriculum that would make contact with elementary-school pupils who were achieving poorly. The results of that effort, called the Elementary School Teaching Project (ESTP), are the subject of this report. Although the approach and the specific goals of the project changed over time, as we shall see, the overall aim remained constant.

Project staff speculated that the best source of materials

[1] "Stirrings in the Big Cities: The Great Cities Projects," reprinted by the Ford Foundation from the *NEA Journal*, LII, No. 4 (April 1963). Other articles appeared in the series "Stirrings in the Big Cities," LI, as follows: Chicago, No. 1 (Jan. 1962); Philadelphia, No. 2 (Feb. 1962); Detroit, No. 3 (March 1962); Pittsburgh, No. 6 (Sept. 1962); and Cleveland, No. 8 (Nov. 1962).

[2] Peter Marris and Martin Rein, *Dilemmas of Social Reform: Poverty and Community Action in the United States* (New York: Atherton Press, 1967).

lay in the experience of successful teachers. After all, there had always been low-income, minority-group youngsters in the classroom, and some had succeeded despite the deficits in their backgrounds. The project sought to discover and inventory the materials and methods developed by the teachers of such children. A staff member described the approach as follows:

> There have always been slum schools and remote rural schools and some innovations have been started in them. In these schools, too, there have always been some teachers who have developed better procedures or more effective instructional materials on their own. The need is to identify these teachers and the better practices they have developed and are using and to help other teachers to learn and to use them too.

Acting on leads in the educational literature, conference reports, and less formal suggestions, staff members visited schools in several states to observe classroom work in progress and discuss with principals and teachers the special problems of teaching such children. During the 1964–65 school year, staff visited some seventy-five schools in which one or more teachers had been identified as particularly effective in teaching. They recorded classroom activity in written notes or on tape.

The staff were looking primarily for effective and innovative teaching practices that could be emulated broadly; content was generally not questioned. Their basic assumption was that the distinctive viewpoints and experiences of many poor, minority children resulted in a style of learning different from that of other students.[3] If socioeconomically

[3] For descriptions of the learning styles of such children, see Frank Riessman, *The Culturally Deprived Child* (New York: Harper & Row, 1962), p. 73; Millard H. Black, "Characteristics of the Culturally Disadvantaged Child," in J. L. Frost and G. R. Hawkes, eds., *The Disadvantaged Child: Issues and Innovations* (Boston: Houghton Mifflin, 1966); and Miriam L. Goldberg, "Adapting Teacher Style to Pupil Differences: Teachers for Disadvantaged Children," *idem*. The last work emphasizes the need to match teaching procedures with learning styles.

different pupils fail to respond to traditional pedagogy, the trouble might lie in the failure to match teaching methodology to pupils' learning styles. To put this in another way, the staff defined as effective teaching those practices that recognized and were adapted to the special learning styles of the children.

It should be evident that the staff began with a theoretical bias: The conviction that the failure-to-learn characteristic of low-income, minority-group pupils is due more to deficiencies in the schools themselves than to deficiencies in the pupil or his environment. This position stems from the experience and observation of staff members and others. In particular, it is a response to the demonstrated failure of many compensatory-education approaches which seek to adjust the pupil to traditional practices.[4] The high rate of failure among dropouts who are persuaded to return to school only to meet the same practices from which they retreated is further evidence of the error of focusing on the product—the pupil—rather than on the process—teaching and the instructional setting.

The staff believed, further, that the mission of the schools is to teach children no matter what their state of readiness. When traditional or conventional practices do not succeed, the school is responsible for finding other means of teaching effectively and, if necessary, for changing its concepts and methods drastically in order to do so. Several months of observation yielded disappointing results.

Although some of the practices observed were more imaginative than the standard methods and seemed to be more effective with non-middle-class learners, when held up to close critical scrutiny they did not appear to be very different from techniques described in popular educational journals, in teacher-training courses, and in instructional bulletins circulated by school systems. More important, even the best of these techniques appeared to be unable to make effective con-

---

[4] See, for example, President Nixon's *Message on Educational Reform*, March 3, 1970.

tact with the students. The content of teaching was often so remote from the children's own lives that it seemed highly irrelevant to them. The use of a methodology matched to the learning style of socioeconomically different children was obviously not enough to bridge the gap between the real world these youngsters knew outside the school and the world they were supposed to learn about, which was utterly unreal to them. Accordingly, the emphasis of the investigation shifted to an examination of the relevance of the content of instruction to the learner.

The staff began by drawing up a list of areas of content that they believed might be of special interest to low-income, minority-group pupils, such as intergroup education and social forces, the learner's self-concept, time relationships, and various materials rooted in the children's culture. The list, based on the staff's own classroom experiences as well as the available research, was sent to school principals with a letter asking them to identify teachers who had worked or planned to work with these content areas.

For the next two months, the staff made a series of observations of teachers singled out by principals, according to the revised guidelines, which stressed content. Again, the results were disappointing. Staff came to realize that working through official school channels greatly limited their findings. When asked for the names of teachers who were getting learning results, most principals cited teachers whose methods and content varied only slightly from the school system's officially prescribed programs. Thus, many teachers with a bent for originality, particularly those who tend to wink at rules in the search for results, were screened out. The political climate of some school systems—including the sensitivity of teachers and administrators to unfavorable publicity regarding the school's treatment of poor children, de facto segregation, and other problems—also made it difficult to get into schools to observe or to engage teachers in experimentation.

The project consequently took another direction. A growing number of educators [5] and social scientists were adopting the position that cognitively oriented materials and lessons were of little interest or relevance to the poor, ethnic-minority pupil. Rather than work toward more relevant materials in the cognitive domain—the realm of the intellect—the staff concentrated their explorations in the realm of affect—the realm of emotion and feeling.

After intensive analysis of the information and observations they had gathered earlier, the staff arrived at the broad conclusion upon which the project's model for the development of relevant content is based: *Significant contact with pupils is most effectively established and maintained when the content and method of instruction have an affective basis.* That is, if educators are able to discover the feelings, fears, and wishes that move pupils emotionally, they can more effectively engage pupils from any background, whether by adapting traditional content and procedures or by developing new materials and techniques.

Further analysis brought the staff *beyond* the conclusion that pupils' concerns should serve as a point of departure for "hooking" poor, minority-group children to traditional content. These concerns, they decided, can be legitimate content *in their own right.* Indeed, much of the learning process itself might be aimed at helping children with their concerns.

Moreover, analysis began to show that many of the fundamental concerns of poor children were shared by children from more privileged families—in fact, by all people, adults and children. In short, the staff came to feel that the project's work with regard to socially and ethnically different students has implications for all learners, although the former remained the focus of the project.

In a search for the principal concerns of children, the staff made additional observations of students in and out of the classroom, recording statements by pupils or teachers that seemed to indicate pervasive concerns of the youngsters. State-

[5] *Inter alia,* Carl Rogers, Abraham Maslow, George Brown, Mark Shedd, Richard Foster, Ronald Lippitt, and various staff members of the National Training Laboratories.

ments were also culled from the professional literature on the "disadvantaged." [6] The staff then drew up a tentative model based on the concerns identified in this manner and designed to help teachers to recognize pupil concerns, use them in selecting and developing content, and devise techniques and procedures enabling students to deal with these concerns.

Even though the project developed along more theoretical and conceptual paths than had been anticipated, the staff retained the objective of offering practical help to professionals in charge of the instruction of low-income, minority-group children. Therefore, the staff solicited reactions to the model and help in refining it during the developmental stage.[7] Aware of gaps and inconsistencies in their own thinking, they also undertook to test and refine the model with children in the classroom.

Thus, while continuing to discuss the model in workshops and visits to school systems and universities, the project staff established a continuing forum in which educational practitioners could test ideas in the field. Participants in the forum, who worked directly with students at various grade levels or with in-service and preservice teachers, allotted time and

[6] The results of the staff's attempt to identify and group the concerns of "disadvantaged" youngsters turned out to coincide closely with the findings of research conducted independently by a number of social psychologists. Among those reporting similar concerns was Jack R. Gibb, who identified "four basic concerns that arise inevitably from all social interaction": acceptance concern ("fears about self-adequacy"), data concern ("a deep sense of depersonalization and isolation"), goal concern ("a loss of identity, a feeling of not knowing who he is or what he wants from life"), and control concern ("a deep feeling that he cannot get himself to do what he wants to do or exert any significant influence on the world of which he is a part"). Leland P. Bradford, Jack R. Gibb, and Kenneth D. Benne, *T-Group Theory and Laboratory Method* (New York: John Wiley, 1964), pp. 280–82.

[7] The staff was cautious in disseminating copies of the model during its early stages, however. We wanted it to evolve into a well-tested instrument for widespread classroom use, not merely a fashionable device whose impact would be spent in workshops, journals, and among the pedagogical cognoscenti (as was the fate of much of the progressive-education movement). These fears were amplified by some uncritical responses to the model and by the tendency of many teachers to adopt it unquestioningly as the solution to immediate problems.

resources to experiment with the model for developing educational programs built on the concerns of learners.[8]

On the basis of suggestions and data supplied by the forum participants, the model went through several stages of development and revision. Despite its state of refinement when the project terminated, the staff regarded it as an instrument that should be continually revised for many years to come. In their own institutions, forum participants and others involved tangentially with the project are continuing to work on several specific areas suggested by the model—for example, techniques for eliciting cues to students' concerns; lessons based on ways in which children judge and evaluate themselves; the role of expectations as they affect self-concept, power, and connectedness; techniques and content that help a child perceive himself and others accurately; instructional games relating to self-identity.

The project that began with the specific short-term goal of observing and disseminating teaching methods that had been used successfully with one group of children has thus evolved into a strategy that may have much broader application—a strategy for generating original content and procedures based upon the concerns of all children. The model, the instrument for this strategy, is neither a panacea nor a whole new curriculum. Rather, it is an approach to a hitherto neglected part of the curriculum that many educators regard as indispensable in meeting the individual educational needs of children and the educational goals of American society.

THE PLAN OF THE BOOK

Before describing an instructional model for a curriculum that we feel would redress the gross imbalance between cognitive and affective content, we turn, in Chapter II, to an analysis of the nature of instruction relevance, the behavioristic goals of education, and the relation between the realms

[8] Members of this field-testing group are listed in the front matter.

of cognition and affect. Chapter III is a detailed presentation of the model developed by ESTP to help teachers in developing, evaluating, and—most important—using a curriculum of affect, based on children's concerns.

Chapters IV through VII illustrate the model in action by presenting informal descriptions of lessons devised and taught by members of the staff and the field-testing unit. None of the exercises, lessons, units, or techniques described here can promise clear-cut results. None of them has been tested exhaustively, and many have been used with only one or two types of children. Only two experiments—"One-Way Glasses" (pp. 77–99) and "Who Are You . . . ?" (pp. 67–71)—illustrate the entire model in sequence; the others illuminate only portions of it. In short, the experiments are independent entities, related only through their common relationship to the model. Rather than serve as a curriculum guidebook, they are presented in the hope that they will encourage educators to try them out and improve them.

Chapter VIII is a verbatim transcript of an interview conducted by Mr. Weinstein with a group of youngsters who had participated in a program that applied the model. Finally, Chapter IX offers some afterthoughts by the editors.

EDITORS' NOTES

When the project described in this report began, the focus was the educational problems of a group known as "the disadvantaged." [9] On at least three grounds, we now believe the designation "disadvantaged" is inaccurate and should be avoided.

First, it was intended to refer to children of low-income status (usually members of racial minorities as well) who performed poorly in school because, it was said, they had been deprived of certain cultural, sensory, and environmental factors believed to be conducive to learning. But the theory

[9] In fact, we are also the authors of a book called *The Disadvantaged: Challenge to Education* (New York: Harper & Row, 1968).

of cultural deprivation and disadvantage is being sharply challenged because its referent is a white, middle-class norm. It implicitly denies value to the experience, culture, and history of members of racial minorities—in particular, blacks, Puerto Ricans, Mexican-Americans, and American Indians. As Andrew Billingsley has pointed out, "To say that a people have no culture is to say that they have no common history which has shaped and taught them. And to deny the history of a people is to deny their humanity." [10]

Second, the word suggests that the burden of failure rests on the shoulders of the students, that it is not the deficiencies of the educational system that are responsible but the fact that vast numbers of minority-group students are incapable of taking advantage of a basically sound system. This position also is being challenged by those who believe that the task of education is, simply, to educate, and to do whatever is necessary to accomplish that objective, regardless of the individual characteristics of the learner.

Third, the word "disadvantaged" implies that the schools are adequately serving the white middle class; yet it has become increasingly clear that many children of this background are also "disadvantaged" by prevailing modes and practices of education.

Therefore, we believe that "disadvantaged" should be relegated to the scrapheap of the euphemisms it was intended to replace ("culturally deprived," "slow learners," and so on). These terms too were coined with good intentions but were found to reflect racial and social-class chauvinism. Today a new concept of disadvantage is being advanced to include everyone who is denied what he needs for fulfillment of his human potential.[11]

The Project effectively ended in 1968, but the preparation and publication of this report were unduly delayed for a number of reasons beyond anyone's control. In the meantime,

[10] *Black Families in White America* (Englewood Cliffs, N.J.: Prentice-Hall, 1969), p. 37.
[11] Fantini and Weinstein, *The Disadvantaged, op. cit.*

many educators have become aware of the importance of constructing educational strategies and tactics in terms of the affective realm. To some, therefore, our discussion and the model for an affectively based curriculum will have a familiar ring.

We suspect that for most, however, the material will be fresh. Moreover, our work makes no pretense to definitiveness. We hope that it will influence individual teachers to re-examine their attitudes and practices in light of affective considerations and that it will stimulate planners and others to explore further the implications of our observations and of the model for relevant education.

2

AFFECT AND
LEARNING

In seeking a point of departure for innovation and reform, two of the major questions educators confront are "What content is most meaningful to youngsters?" and "How can we teach it most effectively?"

The emphasis in education has long been on the means: How can control of the class be achieved and maintained? How can the teacher make contact with the children? And, especially, how does one teach them a particular subject?

Under the impetus of Sputnik, the pendulum of education swung from a long-term preoccupation with methods of teaching to an intense interest in content. The chief result was the curriculum-reform movement of the past decade. The recent recognition of our failure to teach poor, minority-group children, however, has begun to fuse these two interests. Increasingly, educators are realizing that how one goes about teaching is very closely related to what one tries to teach. Experience with the socioeconomically different pupil has made it dramatically clear that no teaching procedure can be effective if the content is of little interest to the class.

LEARNING AND BEHAVIOR

The discrepancy between the behavior of individuals in society and what they have learned, or at least what the schools purport to teach, suggests the need for examination of education's chosen channel for changing or affecting behavior. Traditionally, this channel has been subject matter per se—the courses offered, the curriculum taught, the academic disciplines. A discrepancy exists between subject matter and behavior because the behavioral objectives of education have become submerged, if not obliterated, by narrow subject-matter objectives, which include nothing about the student's behavior and his relations with others. John Goodlad has stated this predicament clearly.

> Little effort has been made to determine the ultimate aims of schooling and the respective contribution each discipline can make to them. Instead, the objectives of schooling have become the composite of the objectives set for each subject. . . . The goals of today's schools do not extend beyond those subjects that have succeeded in establishing themselves in the curriculum.[1]

In most schools today, curriculum is based more on the requirement of the various subject disciplines than on other needs. Rarely is curriculum designed to help the student deal in personal terms with the problems of human conduct.

[1] *The Changing School Curriculum* (New York: Georgian Press, 1966), p. 92.

How can we account for this gap between educational practices and the professed aims of American education? One possible explanation is that the ultimate aims of education are so complex that the practitioner can readily identify only the more immediate objectives of the subject matter. Although a broad-range goal of teaching literature may be to help the child know himself better by developing an understanding of the ways in which man has responded to his experiences in all periods, somehow few literature courses go beyond the immediate objectives of teaching the child to understand plot, character, and theme. Even in some of the more experimental curriculum guides, specific objectives of units read "To enable the student to identify the basic elements of tragedy," or "To enable the student to describe the rhetorical sense implied in a work of literature." [2]

It is easier to teach toward such specific objectives and, more generally, to recognize and deal with the child's need to know how to read, write, compute, and to have some knowledge of his environment than it is to recognize and deal with his need for a satisfying self-definition, for constructive relationships with others, and for some control over what happens to him. The first set of needs is given the overwhelming emphasis in our educational system.

The proper study of curriculum begins with a statement of educational objectives. Let ours be made clear: Education in a free society should have a broad human focus, which is best served by educational objectives resting on a personal and interpersonal base and dealing with students' concerns. This belief rests on philosophical and moral grounds, but it also has plainly practical implications in terms of the price a society pays for negative social behavior—crime, discrimination, tensions, and, ultimately, widespread pathology.

Many educators, decision makers, and citizens do not agree. They feel that it is either impossible or inappropriate for the schools to assume responsibility for a curriculum with an ultimately humanitarian goal. This does not mean that they

[2] *The Detroit Lakes Plan: An Experiment in Curriculum* (Detroit Lakes, Minn.: 1966), from the section on "Approaches to Literature."

are oblivious to the human condition. It may mean that they feel that the school's legitimate business involves no more than the impartation of knowledge and skills and that humanitarian objectives are the responsibility of other institutions in society.

The Elementary School Teaching Project proceeded on the assumption that the broad objectives of American education must include the preparation of students to engage in constructive personal and social behavior. We believe that existing practice is not affecting behavior adequately. We also believe that in today's complex, precarious world a society has little choice but to pursue the path toward humanitarian behavior. Otherwise, no matter how successful its educational system is in teaching the specific stuff of subject matter, the society is likely to decline and decay. The ultimate purpose of this report, therefore, is to search for paths to greater consonance between education and the way in which people might or should behave.

THE NEED FOR RELEVANCE

Poor, mainly urban, mainly minority-group students—the crisis clientele—particularly and poignantly spotlight the widespread failure of education to lead students toward the behavior our society considers desirable. But the problems that confront this group so acutely afflict other groups as well.

One of the most glaring deficiencies in education is lack of contact with the learner. "School is phony—it has nothing to do with life like we know it. The people we read about are all one way—all good or all bad—and so are the things that happen to them." This verdict is typical of the "disadvantaged," but is it so different from the attitude of other groups?

"It all starts in the first grade," states a Harvard freshman from a well-to-do background.

There we are treated to a candy-cane world where all the children in the textbooks are white tots living in suburbia with a dog running around the lawn. When suburban kids find out about the slums, they're apt to get skeptical. When slum kids are taught about a world that has nothing to do with the world in which they live, they have to do the same.[3]

Many teachers and administrators who work with the disadvantaged are hungry for ways to make contact with their pupils, to make education more meaningful to them. They flock to workshops, insititutes, and special training sessions. There they learn a great deal about the nature of the "culturally deprived child," but little about how to meet his needs. One teacher told us,

> I understand my children better now, but I still don't know what to do with them. For example, I learned that one third of my children probably come from broken homes and that this poses severe problems for the growing child. Now that I know this fact, what do I do to teach them better? How is my understanding related to what I'm expected to teach them in social studies, math, science, and the rest?

Most of the instructional prescriptions that have been offered for dealing with students with learning problems take the form of such rudimentary, isolated practices as using "hip" language, role-playing, and stories based on pupils' experiences. The teacher at first finds these practices exciting, but they are of limited utility. He is still left with standard content and methodology, which he senses are not making contact with the learner.

Similarly, attempts to improve standard content—the work of the Biological Sciences Curriculum Study, the Physical Science Study Committee, Educational Services Incorporated, and other contemporary curriculum-reform agencies— have done much to make the process and curriculum struc-

[3] Steven Kelman, "You Force Kids to Rebel," *Saturday Evening Post* (Nov. 19, 1966), p. 12.

ture more significant in terms of academic subjects, but they have not touched the core of the problem: to make the content more *personally* meaningful, especially for the poor, minority-group child.

The current prescriptions fail to make contact, we believe, because they lack intrinsic relevance for many children, and for poor children in particular. To see what is relevant, and how relevance may be achieved, let us examine some causes of irrelevance in education.

1. Failure to match teaching procedures to children's *learning styles.*

The current literature on lower-class children indicates that they learn best in situations that are nonverbal, concrete, inductive, and kinesthetic. If teachers can develop and use techniques geared specifically to the way children learn best, the teaching will bear a degree of relevance no matter what is being taught. Relevance, then, depends in part on *how* one teaches.

2. The use of material that is outside or poorly related to the learner's *knowledge* of his physical realm of experience.

Teaching that relates to an urban child's neighborhood or city, for example, is more relevant to him, and therefore more likely to engage his interest, than teaching exclusively about suburban life or foreign countries. Relevance, then, depends in part on *what* is taught.

3. The use of teaching materials and methods that ignore the learner's *feelings.*

The learner's feelings about his experiences may serve to involve him more deeply in content. For instance, a unit on the city policeman may appear to be relevant because it falls within the experience of urban pupils. But if the learner has a fear of policemen, the selection of such a subject may actually inhibit his learning unless his fears are identified and addressed at the outset. The reasons for tension between police and community residents must be dealt with, beginning perhaps with incidents in the pupils' experience and proceeding more deeply into the role assigned to the police and the work and concerns of individual policemen. In short, contact must be made with the subject matter on the human level.

In order to achieve relevance at the level of students' feelings, the teacher must determine their attitudes about a given subject before moving them into a more analytical or cognitive realm. Later, the teacher may ask the learner to account for particular feelings, to help him begin to analyze them. A skillful teacher can use the learner's feelings about his experiences to lead him into an awareness of his deeper concerns, a step toward the next level of relevance.

4. The use of teaching content that ignores the *concerns* of the learners.

Concerns involve feelings and emotions more deeply than at the third level of relevance. Concerns are the most persistent, pervasive threads of underlying uneasiness the learners have about themselves and their relation to the world. Concerns always engage feelings, but feelings do not always involve corners. For example, a person may have an immediate, spontaneous reaction to another person or experience intense emotion in listening to an orchestral performance without having a concern about either the person or the orchestra. Feeling anger at having one's toe stepped on would be an immediate feeling; anger at hearing criticism of a group to which one belongs represents a feeling so deep-rooted that it probably reflects a concern. Relevance is achieved on this fourth level if the teacher attempts to deal with fundamental questions that people frequently ask themselves, such as "Who am I?" "How do I fit into the scheme of things?" "Why do I feel the way I do?" "Is there something wrong with me?" "Do they think I'm any good?"

Effective teaching utilizes all four levels of relevance. Educators are beginning to adapt their teaching to the first two levels—pupils' learning styles and experiences. What they are not meeting adequately are the third and fourth levels, which constitute the affective domain. Instead of helping children to deal with the questions they ask themselves, the school asks children, "What do we mean by the Common Market?" "How are animals and people different?" They ignore the child's most persistent question: "What does it have to do with *me?*" But unless there is a connection between the knowledge placed before the child and his experiential and emotional framework, the knowledge he gains will matter little to him and will not be likely to contribute to the behavioral aims of education.

It is our general hypothesis that relevance is that which connects the affective, or feeling, aspects and the cognitive, or conceptualizing, aspects of learning. We believe, further, that a better linkage between the affective domain—the learner's concerns—and the practices of the school would reduce the discrepancy between learning and behavior.

AFFECT AND COGNITION

Educators generally define cognition as the act of processing perceived information and developing higher orders of abstraction and conceptualization. Sterling M. McMurrin, former U.S. Commissioner of Education, defines the cognitive and affective functions of teaching as follows:

The cognitive function of instruction is directed to the achievement and communication of knowledge, both the factual knowledge of the sciences and the formal relationships of logic and mathematics—knowledge as both specific data and generalized structure. It is discipline in the ways of knowing, involving perception, the inductive, deductive, and intuitive processes, and the techniques of analysis and generalization. It involves both the immediate grasp of sensory objects and the abstractive processes by which the intellect constructs its ideas and fashions its ideals.

The affective function of instruction pertains to the practical life—to the emotions, the passions, the dispositions, the motives, the moral and esthetic sensibilities, the capacity for feeling, concern, attachment or detachment, sympathy, empathy, and appreciation.[4]

But how does the relation between the cognitive and affective functions affect motivation and learning? Affect is not only intense feeling or emotion; it is also an expression of the basic forces that direct and control behavior. In the affective domain "the most influential controls are to be found." That domain "contains the forces that determine the nature of an individual's life and ultimately the life of an entire people."[5] Many of these forces, such as the inner need for a positive self-concept, power, connectedness, and so on, have been made more salient by the current focus on the rights and status of minority groups. These are the intrinsic drives that motivate behavior.

In urging that the teacher vigorously explore the affective domain we are not asserting its primacy over cognition or erecting a wall between cognition and affect. Indeed, cognitive learning is a natural way of becoming more capable of dealing with one's inner needs. The more analytic the person, the more means he presumably has available for dealing with his feelings and concerns. Consequently, cognitive machinery should link inner needs to the environment and provide the organism with means of coping with the requirements of the environment.

As Dr. George I. Brown suggests

. . . it might help to talk about "harmony" between affect and cognition in the sense that within the on-going growth of the individual, often the affective domain has become anesthetized, or feelings can be going in a different direction from the cognitive knowing: The intent is to get a

[4] "What Tasks for the Schools?" *Saturday Review* (Jan. 14, 1967), p. 41.
[5] David R. Krathwohl, Benjamin S. Bloom, and Bertram B. Masia, *Taxonomy of Educational Objectives* (New York: David McKay, 1956), p. 91.

harmony between the two so that they both go in the same direction.[6]

But the educational system does not foster harmony between affect and cognition; it usually emphasizes cognition at the expense of affect. The reasons are both operational and policy-based. It is less demanding to teach for cognitive than for affective objectives, and it is far less difficult to grade student achievement in the cognitive realm. A more fundamental reason, however, is the prevalent feeling that the student's beliefs, attitudes, feelings, and concerns are private and should not be dealt with in the school. As Krathwohl has remarked

Our own society has fluctuated as to the affective objectives it will permit the school to develop. Political and social forces are constantly at work, pressing the schools for some affective objectives and just as constantly placing restrictions on the school with regard to others. The play of these forces has, in many instances, made teachers and school administrators wary of expressing these objectives and all too frequently has led school staffs to retreat to the somewhat less dangerous cognitive domain.[7]

For these reasons, the school severely restricts attempts to link cognition and affect to the use of such elements as play, classroom climate, readiness, teacher-pupil interaction, and motivation as means of encouraging the learner to accept prescribed content. For example, a young child who appears to be emotionally unready to read is not forced into a structured reading program but is placed in a "reading readiness" program, which capitalizes on his interests as a way of facilitating his learning of content. Similarly, the teacher may use children's fear of doctors as a basis for developing a unit on "Our Community Friends—the Doctor, Dentist, and Nurse."

[6] From a letter to the authors by George I. Brown, Professor of Education, University of California, Santa Barbara, May 12, 1967.
[7] Krathwohl et al., op. cit., p. 90.

Popular music or current slang may be used to introduce a unit on poetry. In these examples, fear or slang is not regarded as content worthy of attention in itself; rather, it is used as a "hook" for the institutionalized cognitive content —the subject matter. All instructional roads seem to lead to cognition as the end product. But, as we have noted, cognition makes scant contribution to the broader behavioral objectives of education.

. . . our preference for approaching affective achievement through the attainment of cognitive objectives tends to focus attention on these cognitive goals as ends in themselves without our determining whether they are actually serving as means to an affective end.[8]

Today cognitive processes and content are riding the peak of the educational wave. Cognitive development is equated with mastery of institutionally prescribed content, with "understanding of" or "knowledge about" a variety of *academic* subjects, rather than understanding or knowledge of how these subjects can serve the needs of the student. The entire machinery of the school, including its reward system, reflects this stance; grades, promotion, recognition, and so on are based on the degree of mastery of the cognitive. In fact, the operational definition of learning used in the school is a cognitive definition. The classical notion of learning as a "change in behavior" is commonly interpreted by our schools to mean a change in cognitive behavior, measured by paper-and-pencil tests and verbalization. Catalogues and research reports from many schools of education indicate that this emphasis on change in cognitive behavior is reinforced by much of the teaching in educational psychology and research in learning.

Yet, as we noted at the outset, cognitive understanding does not guarantee behavior in harmony with the understanding. Studies of the relationship between academic achieve-

[8] *Ibid.*, p. 57.

ment and performance in later life point to the same conclusion. Holland and Richards conclude from their own and earlier investigations that "studies of academic and non-academic potential and achievement have little relationship to other kinds of non-academic potential and socially important performance.[9]

Why does the cognitive orientation not affect behavior directly? In that it encourages (or requires) the individual to reconstruct reality symbolically or abstractly, cognition is removed from the real and disconnected from the feeling level of learning. Dewey described the experiential level of learning as follows.

To "learn from experience" is to make a backward and forward connection between what we do to things and what we enjoy or suffer from things in consequence. Under such conditions, doing becomes a trying; an experiment with the world to find out what it is like; the undergoing becomes instruction—discovery of the connection of things. . . . Experience is primarily an active-passive affair; it is not primarily cognitive.[10]

The pervasive emphasis on cognition and its separation from affect poses a threat to our society in that our educational institutions may produce cold, detached individuals, uncommitted to humanitarian goals. Certainly, a modern society cannot function without ever increasing orders of cognitive knowledge. Yet knowledge per se does not necessarily lead to desirable behavior. Knowledge can generate feeling, but it is feeling that generates action. For example, we may know all about injustice to minorities in our society, but until we feel strongly about it we will take little action.

[9] John L. Holland and James M. Richards, Jr., "Academic and Non-Academic Accomplishment: Correlated or Uncorrelated?" *ACT Research Reports*, No. 2 (April 1965), p. 20. See also Krathwohl *et al.*, *op. cit.*, p. 20.
[10] John Dewey, *Democracy and Education* (New York: Macmillan, 1964), p. 140. (Originally published in 1916.)

A link to the affective, or emotional, world of the learner is therefore necessary. *Unless knowledge is related to an affective state in the learner, the likelihood that it will influence behavior is limited.*

Yet, as we have noted, the spiral is usually reversed: The areas of affect are prescribed—often severely limited and narrowly defined—by the cognitive, in order to serve the cognitive. With the affective in this subordinate position, it is unlikely, or at best coincidental, that knowledge will influence behavior.

THE AFFECTIVE AS RELEVANT CONTENT

Concerns, wants, interests, fears, anxieties, joys, and other emotions and reactions to the world contain the seeds of "motivation." Dealing with the child's inner concerns constitutes recognition of, and respect for, him. By validating his experiences and feelings, we tell the child, in essence, that he *does* know something. Probably this is the most important factor in linking relevant content with self-concept. For when the teacher indicates to the child in effect that the experience he brings with him has nothing to do with the "worthwhile" knowledge that the school intends to set before him, he is, without realizing it, telling the child in effect that *he* is worthless, for he *is* his experience.

It is not surprising that when teachers do talk about the real problems students are facing, there is a marked change in attentiveness. At such times the teacher generally thinks, "We're digressing, let's get back to work." Suppose that several students interrupt a social studies lesson to tell of a fight they saw on the subway between a policeman and a young boy. They say that the boy, who had tried to break away, was slapped several times. They think this is unfair and wouldn't like it to happen to them. A social studies lesson could be given great relevance if the teacher treated this experience not as a digression but as legitimate content in its own right. Information about the city's system of law enforcement would become personally meaningful if it could be tied directly to the incident and to the students' own concerns about powerlessness.

The reason students' motivation is higher during such "digressions" than during regular lessons is that they can relate what they are learning cognitively to their own concerns. Moreover, their subsequent behavior is more likely to be affected directly by the learning that takes place. Relevance, then, becomes a matter of functionally linking extrinsic curricula to basic intrinsic concerns and feelings.

Our observations lead us to the conclusion that schools ignore the affective domain as content and instead assume that students will be motivated to learn an extrinsic body of content if enough pressure is placed upon them. Although many pupils make the adjustment, some educators are beginning to question whether the costs are not excessive. For one thing, many learners who adjust to the pressure end up regarding formal education as an exercise to be tolerated or a system to be beaten. For another, the pressure to adjust and succeed, exerted especially by parents, often produces emotional tensions in students that result in antisocial behavior in adolescence or later in life. In either case, learning is too often regarded, even by students who are adept at adjusting to the pressures, as forced and unnatural. And, finally, it is the "disadvantaged" who are least likely to have the environmental and psychic resources with which to adjust.

THE THREE-TIER CURRICULUM

The model for an affective curriculum suggested in Chapter III is only one approach to the problems of content relevance and behavioral dissonance. It is advanced as a means of redressing an imbalance—of filling vital areas that the traditional educational system has ignored—rather than as a replacement for all areas of curriculum. Its place in a total school curriculum may be illustrated by visualizing the school in terms of three tiers, or curricular modes.[11]

One tier is comprised of reading, computation, and writing skills, among others; basic information in the social studies, science, language, and other disciplines; and major concepts of specific disciplines—the generally acknowledged essential building blocks for the intellectual development of the child. This tier serves as an information and skills-retrieval base. It is also the mode that lends itself best to individually paced, materials-centered, and automated instruction. Most current discussion of individualized and programmed instruction is directed to this tier.

The second tier, or curricular mode, consists of drawing latent talents and abilities from the learner. Joyce terms this the idiosyncratic or "personal discovery" tier. Like the first tier, it is highly individualized, and it calls for the development of individual creativity and the exploration of interests —everything from learning to play a tuba to working on a research project of a student's own design to writing a play.

The third tier may be thought of as a group-inquiry curriculum. It consists mainly of societal issues and problems that are related to the self and an exploration of self and others—not in the sense of individual emotional problems but in terms of the thread of *commonality* that runs through these personal issues. Exploration of a common concern— world hunger, pollution, racial injustice—should lead to individual self-examination in terms of the effects of a common issue on oneself and the possible courses of action in dealing with the issue. Inherent in this tier is the development of the individual's own personality, his skill in interpersonal relations, and the awareness skills of identifying, articulating, and evaluating his own feelings, concerns, and opinions and comparing them with those of others in a group. It is here that the curriculum of concerns would fit most readily. Al-

[11] We are indebted to Dr. Bruce R. Joyce for his insight in describing a school with three curricular modes, in *Restructuring Elementary Education: A Multiple Learning Systems Approach* (New York: Teachers College, Columbia University, 1966), p. 4. For a more detailed account of this organizational pattern, see Mario D. Fantini and Gerald Weinstein, *Making Urban Schools Work* (New York: Holt, Reinhart & Winston, 1968).

though the affective may be used in any of the tiers to facilitate connection to the learning process, it is in this third tier, and possibly in the second tier, that it can become fully developed content in its own right.

In a school using all three curricular modes effectively, none would be isolated; each would overlap and interlock with the others. For example, the group-inquiry tier could not function adequately without dipping into the basic skills-and-information tier.[12]

Reading, writing, and oral expression—that is, the communications skills generally—are important as means of self-discovery and development of interests (the second tier), and for exploration of societal issues (the third tier). Mathematics, history, economics, and science—virtually all subject matter—are functionally necessary at various points throughout the curriculum. As Joyce explains, "Each of these curricular modes has advantages for some educational purposes and severe limitations for others. Blended together in proper proportions, they can achieve a far greater and a more balanced educational result than can any one of them taken alone."[13] We recommend a curriculum of concerns as an ingredient to be blended with other curricular modes, not as a "wall-to-wall curriculum."

To summarize, then, our present educational system gives highest priority to cognitive content and regards other content areas merely as instruments for getting to prescribed cognitive content. The prevailing assumption is that by mastering cognitive content, the individual learns to behave appropriately as a citizen in an open society. We question the validity of this assumption that extrinsic subject matter alone can lead to humanitarian behavior—that is, whether the cognitive man is necessarily the humanitarian man.

Our proposal is to reverse the direction of the prevailing cognitive emphasis. We suggest that knowledge alone does not adequately produce the behavior necessary to such a so-

12 Joyce, op. cit., p. 3.
13 Ibid.

ciety. The chances of affecting behavior will be greater if the learner's feelings and concerns are recognized and made to direct the cognition that logically should follow and if cognition is used to help the learner cope with his concerns.

For the so-called disadvantaged in particular, but for all children generally, we believe that the affective realm contains intrinsic forces for motivation and, consequently, may have greater impact on behavior and on realizing human potential. We regard cognition and affect as complementary, not contradictory, forces. They have not played balanced roles in education because affect has received such meager recognition, experimentation, and practice. Krathwohl and his colleagues refer to the affective domain as a Pandora's box: "To keep the 'box' closed is to deny the existence of the powerful motivational forces that shape the life of each of us. To look the other way is to avoid coming to terms with the real."[14]

Affect can serve not only to revivify elements of the old subject matter but also, and primarily, to open vistas for new subject matter.

Chapter III focuses on the development of an analytic instructional model that may enable teachers to work in the affective realm and thereby generate more relevant content and procedures. We suggest that a curriculum based on the children's concerns not only will be more relevant but also will be a step toward answering the problems of human conduct.

[14] Krathwohl et al., op. cit., p. 91.

3

A MODEL FOR DEVELOPING A CURRICULUM OF AFFECT

The model we shall present in this chapter is an instrument for helping teachers to generate new content and techniques and to assess the relevance of existing curriculum, content, and techniques. It outlines a way of linking affect with cognition so that cognition can be used to help the learner cope with his concerns. In that sense it is a model for a "curriculum of affect."

The model is presented diagrammatically as a series of steps for ordering, integrating, and interrelating aspects and inputs of teaching and learning. As is true of most schematic presentations of intellectual and psychological processes, the "steps" or aspects of the model are not distinct from one another but overlap more often than not. The components are

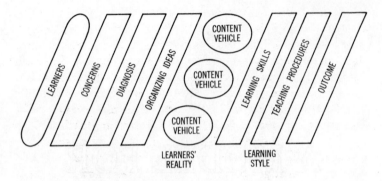

isolated in the diagram and in the following discussion to enable teachers to see how a given practice is related to the process as a whole and to other components.

IDENTIFYING THE LEARNING GROUP

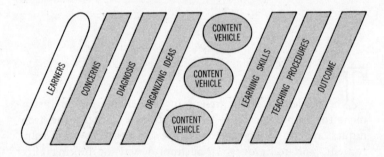

The first step in determining appropriate content and teaching procedures for a curriculum geared to learners' needs and concerns is to identify the learners as a group as precisely as possible. What proves to be effective with a given class will depend to a large extent on the developmental (age), economic (lower, middle, or upper income), geographic (rural or urban; northern, southern), cultural, and racial or ethnic characteristics of the children. Whether a given group is comprised of urban Negroes, Puerto Ricans, rural whites, children of migrant workers, Mexican-Americans, or American Indians (of a given tribe), for example, may be quite as important as the fact that all the children are from poor families.

The emphasis on group characteristics and concerns differentiates this model from other affective approaches, most of which concentrate on highly individualized emotional problems. We believe that since most children are taught in groups, knowledge of their common interests and characteristics is a prerequisite to differentiated diagnosis and individualized teaching.

Even if a teacher finds more than one sociological grouping in his class, as is often the case, it is not necessary to develop two or more entirely distinct curricula. He may want to provide somewhat different instruction for each group, but there will be certain commonalities that can be utilized with all of the groups. It should be evident in the following discussion that the concerns discussed are shared by all children, although they are manifested quite differently by different groups.

IDENTIFYING SHARED CONCERNS

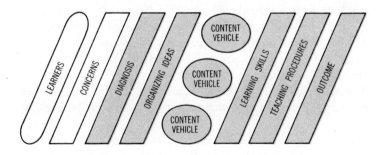

It is the premise of this book that the concerns of the learners should be a major factor in determining the basic organizing elements, concepts, generalizations, and content areas of the curriculum; the teaching procedures used; and the desired outcomes of the teaching-learning process. What is taught and how it is taught should ultimately help the pupils to deal more effectively with their concerns. An essential step, then, is to identify those concerns and to distinguish them from more superficial and transitory feelings.

Interests and Concerns

The curriculum of concerns is not a new version of the child-centered approach of the progressive-education era. Reformers of that earlier day championed teaching based on the "needs and interests" of youngsters. In practice, however, teaching followed "interests" far more than "needs." For one thing, interests were more easily adapted as vehicles for leading the learner into cognitive content. For another, a pedagogical response to needs would mean that teachers and the school would have to grapple with problems for which there are no ready answers. Then, as now, educators were reluctant to enter such areas.

Progressive educators were on the right track in sensing the link between interests and needs, on the one hand, and learning, on the other. But their preoccupation with interests and their reluctance to deal with needs led to misunderstandings—and often ridicule. Teachers who subscribed to the principle of interest-centered instruction sought to strengthen their pupils' motivation for learning by assessing the pupils' interests and building programs based on them. If the children were interested in cars, that was what they studied. If they were interested in animals, a study of animals was used as a springboard from which to initiate a unit on farm products.

But the concept of building curriculum wholly on a base of the learners' interests is limited. First, it is confined to present interests; it shuts out matters in which learners might some day be interested. Second, what pupils, especially young pupils, say interests them may not be what really *concerns* them. For example, a teacher told the project staff that her class had an almost compulsive interest in science. Asked "What aspect of science?" she replied, "Evaporation—the children seem utterly intrigued by evaporating water." Upon questioning the pupils, however, we found that it was not evaporation as such that fascinated the class but, rather, a concern with change and permanence; they were saying, in effect, "If water can disappear, can we?" Similarly, the interest expressed by many boys in racing cars or athletes may actually indicate a concern with power and control.

The fundamental differences between concerns and interests must be understood if affective curricula are to become more than simplistic attempts to capitalize on surface indications of students' feelings. Interests usually are less anxiety-laden than concerns, and they are more likely to be transitory. The term "concerns," as we are using it, connotes an inner uneasiness. Concerns are deeper and more persistent than interests. A person may have an interest (in, say, urban poverty) and yet not be concerned; on the other hand, his interests may give clues to his concerns. Moreover, as we have pointed out earlier, concerns go beyond "feelings," which do not necessarily arouse the frustration or anxiety associated with concerns. An affective curriculum, then, must regard interests as only superficial clues to the roots of uneasiness or anxiety in the learner.

Concerns may be positive, of course, rooted in aspirations and desires that are seeking outlets. But all concerns are negative in the sense that they signify disequilibrium or incomplete satisfaction—the gap between reality and an ideal. The curriculum should deal with ways of helping students to work toward achieving their aspirations as well as toward overcoming fears and anxieties.

Clues to Pupil Concerns

In seeking to identify the common concerns of youngsters in his classroom, the teacher may search for clues in the professional literature, the folklore of various groups, discussions with colleagues, and, of course, his own observation of his students. Concerns may manifest themselves nonverbally, and these clues are far more subtle and difficult for teachers to interpret than students' verbal expressions. The most valuable and direct indications, however, are found in what the learners themselves say or write about their lives and their relations with the world. What the children say may lead to an understanding of how they are dealing with their concerns as well as to what the concerns are. The frequency of clues is a significant indication of whether the problem reflects fleeting feeling or a deep and persistent concern. The teacher, therefore, should keep track of how often a particular clue appears.

The following statements, supplied by teacher-trainers, are typical of remarks made by students from urban ghettos.

Why do *I* live in the slums? [*After a teacher had taken a group of children on a bus tour of the community, including the more affluent neighborhoods*]

Listen, see if this is right. I'm here to get educated, right? You're educated—so it's like you're telling me I've gotta be like you. Now, if I've gotta become like you, it means that what I am now isn't too good. So what I want to know is, how much of me do I have to give up to become educated? [*By a scholarship college student to his professor*]

Whenever I leave Harlem I feel like a fish out of water.

I think about what I should do when I get out of school and I just don't know. The people in my neighborhood, in Harlem, or downtown, they're all doing it wrong. And if one tries to get out, the rest laugh. Like they say that they tried and couldn't do it, so you're not going to do it either. And this guy feels, "Well, maybe I can't do it," and he comes back to the slums. You figure, you know, they failed, man, and I might as well give up . . . and that's the thing that gives a feeling of inferior. It tells a person that no matter how hard they try they can't get out. That's the whole thing right there.[1]

Educators can develop situations and procedures to stimulate pupil-teacher interaction and prompt similar expressions of concerns. A few such techniques are described in Chapters IV through VII.

Three Major Concerns

From various sources of clues to pupil concerns, project staff concluded that most of these concerns fall into one of three broad classifications.

1. Concern about *self-image*. ("I may be brown, but I'm not black!" "How can you like me when I don't like myself?" "We're the dumb special class!" [2]

2. Concern about *disconnectedness;* a wish to establish a connection with others or with society at large, to know where one fits in the scheme of things. ("Why should I listen to my parents? Look at the way they live!" "In order for me to get educated I gotta be like you? What about me?" "You can't trust nobody, white or Negro.")

3. Concern about *control* over one's life. ("It's no use trying, there's nothing you can do about it." "I'm Hercules, I can do anything." "What the hell can I do? This is the attitude; we can do nothing, so leave it alone. People think you're always going to be under pressure from the white man and he owns and runs everything, and we are so dependent on him that there's nothing I can do. This is the general impression I've gotten from most of the adults in Harlem.")

Although there may well be other concerns that would legitimately fall within the province of education, we have chosen only three major patterns, for several reasons. In the sample of children's statements to which the project had

[1] Charlotte Leon Mayerson (ed.), *Two Blocks Apart: Juan Gonzales and Peter Quinn* (New York: Holt, Rinehart & Winston, 1965), p. 104.

[2] Note that all of these statements might have been made by middle-class children as well as by the so-called disadvantaged.

access, these three were the most frequently expressed aside from physical concerns, such as shelter and safety, with which schools are not directly involved. They also recur in a wide variety of sociopsychological theories of needs.[3] Finally, they are broadly inclusive; at one time or another during the course of the analysis, the staff tentatively put forward other major concerns, only to conclude that they were actually parts of the three basic patterns. It should be pointed out that the settings in which the statements were made aided in their interpretation and grouping (for example, the feelings of disconnectedness experienced by a student reared on an Indian reservation will differ from those of a Harlem Negro) and that several of the statements imply a combination of concerns.

The problems with which these children are grappling are rooted in the core of their being. They are questions that most people face, but for children, particularly those low on the socioeconomic ladder, they are enormously powerful.

DIAGNOSING UNDERLYING FACTORS

Although different groups of children may have identical concerns, the *manifestations* of these concerns may differ depending on the social forces affecting the children. For example, the clue to a low-income-minority child's concern for power might be his statement: "So what if I graduate from high school? I won't get a good job anyway." An advan-

[3] Henry A. Murray, in *Explorations in Personality* (New York: Oxford University Press, 1938), pp. 80–85 and 109–15, develops a list of more than twenty-five needs, including power, affection, and status. David C. McClelland, J. W. Atkinson, R. A. Clark, and E. L. Lowell, in *The Achievement Motive* (New York: Appleton-Century-Crofts, 1953), discuss three needs: achievement, affiliation, and power. J. B. Potter, in *Social Learning and Clinical Psychology* (Englewood Cliffs, N.J.: Prentice-Hall, 1954), lists six need areas. Abraham H. Maslow, in *Motivation and Personality* (New York: Harper & Row, 1954), lists seven. Regardless of the number of needs each of these and other researchers list, most of them include needs similar to the three concern patterns noted above.

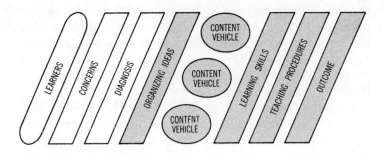

taged child might express a similar concern by taking a driver-education course.[4]

Even within the same group there may be varying manifestations of the same concern. For example, a northern urban Negro might act out all three concerns less passively and express them in more "hip" language than a southern rural Negro. The reasons for the same concern also may differ. The northern Negro's greater aggressiveness in his concern for identity, for example, may be due to the greater frustration and insecurity he experiences because the lines of discrimination are more disguised in the North than in the South, to his relatively greater freedom to express aggression, or to the fact that his aspirations have received (at least on an overt level) greater support. This variance within the group termed "disadvantaged" highlights the need, noted earlier, to describe and differentiate the learner group as specifically as possible.

On the other hand, different groups may express a concern in an identical manner. The statement "It's no use trying, there's nothing you can do about it" expresses a concern for power, whether the speaker is poor or well-to-do. The reasons for feeling powerless may differ, of course, and so may the reactions to powerlessness.

These and other psychosociological forces underlying the

[4] *Sixteen in Webster Groves,* a CBS film study of an affluent suburb of St. Louis, quoted a student as follows: "There is one place where your life is almost your own. And that's behind the steering wheel of a car."

concern patterns discussed above must be recognized and understood if the teacher is to develop a curriculum that meets the pupils' concerns. Diagnosis of these forces should, of course, focus on the distinctive *group* manifestations of concerns. Why are certain manifestations of concerns characteristic of a particular group of learners?

Granting that societal factors affect manifestations of concern, can the teacher build a curriculum adapted to his pupils' concerns by beginning with the pupils' *statements* of concerns, without diagnosing them? We think not, as the following example shows.

Consider the previously quoted statement, "It's no use trying, there's nothing you can do about it." Analysis of such a statement made by a middle-class child might disclose that he lives in an overprotected situation; everything has been done for him, he has not been called upon to make decisions, and he has been told in many ways that he is too inexperienced to make them. On the basis of such a diagnosis, the teacher might develop procedures that would allow the child to make the kind of *individual* decisions that will help him to develop confidence. Had the teacher acted on the statement without the sociological diagnosis, he might have developed procedures that allowed the child to work initially in a group on group decisions, since groups very often are more effective in "doing something about it." This prescription, however, would deny the child the opportunity to make his own decisions.

The same statement made by a poor child might reflect a *lack* of protection and strong support; such a child might feel helpless because he has been left on his own too much. Diagnosis of his concern might suggest teaching procedures that would allow him to work with others and thereby acquire greater confidence. As a result, he might come to realize eventually that he, individually, can affect his own life. Without diagnosis, the teacher might mistakenly decide on the basis of the statement that the youngster was passive and needed encouragement to stand on his own two feet and assert himself—precisely what his environment had forced him to do all along, contributing to his feelings of powerlessness. In both cases, the general explanation might be the same—both pupils have been "acted upon" so much as to make them feel helpless and less than worthwhile as a person —but the approach to increasing their sense of self-worth would differ as a result of the diagnosis.

Failure to diagnose societal forces correctly can lead not only to misguided teaching procedures, as in this example, but also to the selection of inappropriate teaching content, themes, and objectives. Take, for example, a typical "slow" class, in which the children have said that they think they are "dumb." If the class contains many members of a minority group and if the teacher does not bother to determine why the pupils think they are stupid, he may conclude that they feel this way because they belong to a minority group. Let us assume that the reason for their feeling is that the *organization of the school* (perhaps the fact that they are grouped together) has given them very little opportunity to succeed. In this case, the important societal factor is not class or caste, but a social institution—the school. On the assumption that the students are suffering from feelings of racial inferiority, the teacher may give them material to read on the theme that all racial groups have the same intellectual capacities. But this message may be nullified by the students' continuing feeling that they are stupid because they cannot read the material. If the teacher can discern the actual reason for their feeling, he will select materials and concepts on an altogether different theme, perhaps raising such questions as "How do people judge themselves?" "How does the school affect your own judgment of yourself?" and "Is the school's judgment of you always accurate?"

THE BEHAVIORAL OUTCOMES

As we have said, the teaching process should lead to certain behavioral changes in the learner. The outcomes the staff considers desirable are more congruent with the broad aims of education than are most specific subject-matter objectives. For example, if a learner says, "I see that I can do more

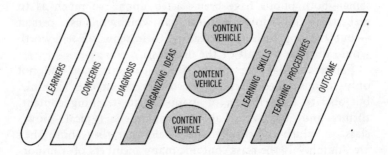

things than I ever thought I could," we would conclude that the teaching process has met the general educational aim of fulfilling human potential.

The behavioral changes to which teaching procedures should be directed are suggested by diagnosis of the learners' concerns, principally as expressed in their statements. The desired outcome should be described in terms of behavior indicating that it has been achieved. Thus one does not teach "power" directly to a group characterized by feelings of powerlessness. Instead, the teacher asks, "What would a given child say or do if he felt more powerful that he isn't saying or doing now?" The teacher would then describe behavior that gives evidence of increased feelings of control— not only in the sense of power over others but also in the sense of power to affect circumstances or to do something *for* people (the latter, of course, related to the concern for connection with others as well).[5]

For example, evidence of a person's sense of power is seen

[5] The concept of service to others as a source of a feeling of potency is vividly described in George Besseler, "The Content Is the Medium: The Confidence Is the Message," *Psychology Today* (Jan. 1968), pp. 32–35. A headnote to the article states, "There are ten kindergarten children sitting with their teacher in a circle while one boy talks about something he did yesterday that made his mother feel very good. For a moment, if you walked into this classroom, you might think you were eavesdropping on the usual 'show and tell,' but only for a moment. It would become obvious very quickly that the little boy is showing himself, his teacher, and his classmates that he has power."

in his ability to plan and develop a variety of strategies for overcoming obstacles, in his knowledge of a variety of sources to tap, reorganize, and manipulate in order to get things done. He demonstrates feelings of control by trying and persisting through alternate routes. He makes statements such as "Let's try it this way" or "Let's figure out how to do it" rather than "It's no use, nobody can do anything." He is realistic about what is achievable alone or in a group.

Affirmative change in self-concept is another behavioral outcome that can be gauged by children's statements, as in the following description.

Starting Point	*Desired Outcome*
Statements and behavior that indicate acceptance of inferiority. For example:	Statements and behavior that indicate a sense of pride in certain aspects of uniqueness. For example:
"We're dumb."	I Am Special [6]
"You have to be stupid or crazy to be in this class."	My eyes are special. My hair is special. I feel special. I was made special. I was born special.
	Jerry R.

In assessing the outcomes through learners' statements, the teacher must distinguish between the student's verbalized knowledge of the objective (which commonly echoes what the teacher has said or what the child has read in textbooks) and verbalization about his own feelings. The poem "I Am Special," for example, was judged by both the classroom teacher and the field staff to be a genuine outcome based on real feeling. A crude example of a synthetic response would be the pat answer "Yes" to the teacher's question, "Do you ever feel that you are special?"

[6] Written by a fifth-grade student at P.S. 1, New York City, and reported by his teacher, Mrs. Luci Burrows.

Sometimes the goal may be to have different groups of children express the same outcome differently. Suppose, for example, that we are working toward reducing dependence on others' judgments in the formation of self-concept. We might want a Negro pupil to say something of this sort: "I realize now that I'm not a second-class citizen just because I'm black. I see now that society has made me think that for years. I'm beginning to see that these definitions are not always accurate." We might want a white pupil whose self-concept has previously included a racially based sense of superiority to say, as one did: "I've always been taught that because I'm white or expect to go to Vassar I'm the cream of the crop. That's the idea you come out with—just like when you come out of the ghetto thinking you're a second-class citizen—we come out of our background thinking we're first-rate citizens, and *that's* not necessarily true. I want to feel valuable because I'm *me* rather than because of my circumstances."

Before we discuss procedures for achieving outcomes, it should be noted that the strategy embodied in this model does not seek to *change* concerns directly and immediately but, rather, tries to change the behavior representing the child's way of dealing with his concerns. More important than labeling the concerns, then, is identifying their behavioral manifestations. It is not enough for the teacher to determine curriculum on the basis of his awareness of children's feelings of powerlessness or weak self-image. He must also identify and work with the manner in which groups of children express the concerns, even with their irrational and destructive ways of dealing with concerns. He must encourage constructive techniques; then he can go further and determine the kinds of information, the experiences and concepts, that could help them to handle the concern more effectively.

THE ORGANIZING IDEAS

"Cognitive organizers" can be defined as generalizations, fundamental ideas, principles, and concepts around which

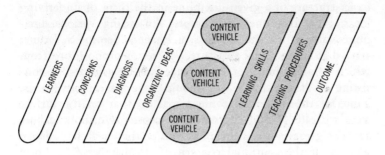

specific curriculum content can be developed. They are the threads with which content and procedures are woven. Since this is a model for a curriculum of concerns, organizing ideas must be selected on the basis of the concerns of the learner rather than academic subject matter, and they must help the learner to cope with his concerns.

The need for such organizing ideas is clear. Many excellent lessons developed by teachers conclude without indicating a way of moving to another level of instruction. They lack a central theme to connect one lesson or unit (much less year) to another. For example, the teacher may succeed in encouraging children to express themselves but, lacking an organizing idea, may fail to utilize this opportunity to impart learning. This suggests the need for ideas—"hooks" —with which to order the variety of experiences provided for the children and to utilize their feedback more effectively.

Organizing ideas, especially those that cut across disciplinary lines, are the most generative and transferable items in the educational process. A concept such as "Man learns to judge his own worth on the basis of certain cultural factors that may or may not be reasonable and accurate" can have more impact on learners who are concerned about self-identity and can be used in more subject areas than a social-studies generalization such as "Men are interdependent."

Appropriate organizing ideas may be borrowed from new curricular developments which attempt to communicate the basic structure of a given discipline in the form of underlying ideas, generalizations, or concepts. Analyzing various disciplines rather than the concerns of learners, Jerome S. Bruner arrived at an "optimal structure," a "set of propositions from which a larger body of knowledge can be generated," consisting of "those things that should have the capacity in the hands of the learner to connect matters that on the surface seem separate," [7] and "spiraling concepts," which he defines as "the great issues, principles, values that a society deems worthy of the continual concern of its members." [8] These may, in terms of this model, be used as organizing ideas.

Discipline-based concepts, again, must be validated in terms of the learner's concerns—that is, in terms of whether they facilitate inquiry into the learner's problems and help him to confront and cope with them. This reverses the traditional approach, in which the subject-matter discipline dictates which generalizations or ideas are most important. Our model, rather, ranks generalizations on the basis of their utility in linking the concerns with desired outcomes.

Consider a teacher who knows that his students are concerned about self-identification because of their statements equating color with negative feelings. He might seek a number of related ideas which will help the students to deal more effectively with color and self-definition. These ideas might include the following:

—The way we see ourselves is learned.

—What we feel and learn about ourselves depends partly upon where we live and who else lives there.

—What we learn may be inaccurate.

—When we belong to a minority group, our perception of ourselves tends to be inaccurate because society's definitions of our group tend to be inaccurate (for example, "Black is bad").

On the basis of his diagnosis of the pupils' manifestations

---

[7] *Toward a Theory of Instruction* (Cambridge, Mass.: Belknap Press of Harvard University Press, 1966), p. 41.
[8] *The Process of Education* (New York: Vintage Books, 1960), p. 52.

of concerns, the teacher could develop a repertory of more specific organizing ideas from various disciplines. For example, from psychology and sociology

1) To know who you are it is necessary to be aware of how you are defining yourself (a) in terms of your own society and culture, (b) in terms of wider groups and values, and (c) in terms of your own individual criteria.

2) The behavior of individuals is related to the structure and organization of the group in which they are placed. The same individual may exhibit a range of roles in different groups to which he belongs.[9]

3) Our expectations depend on what we think will be the *future* consequences between ourselves and a given objective. Expectations also rest upon recollections of similar experiences in the past. Expectations influence the way we think and act.[10]

Some organizing ideas, because of the form in which they are stated, are more immediately operational than others. Many general ideas are not functional until they are applied closely to the experience, understanding, and *language* of the children. Thus, the first organizing idea listed above ("To know who you are . . .") would be more operational if it were reworded, simplified, and broken down as follows:

1) You use people, things, and events to tell you who you are.

2) Some people, things, and events are more important to you than others.

3) The most important ones are those you use most often in judging yourself.

[9] Condensed from the Report of the State Central Committee on Social Studies, California State Department of Education, Sacramento (Nov. 1959), p. 105.
[10] Paraphrased from Anselm L. Strauss, *Mirrors and Masks* (New York: The Free Press, 1959), p. 23.

4) It is important to know what you are using to measure your own self-worth.
5) Certain things, people, and events are important to you because of (a) where you live and who else lives there, (b) what you think is good for people, and (c) the fact that you are you.

CONTENT VEHICLES

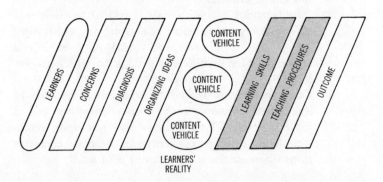

What content will most directly relate the learners' concerns and the organizing ideas to the outcomes? The model's concept of "content" is broad in order to give the teacher a wide range of choice. Content vehicles may include not only the conventional subject areas (English, social studies, mathematics, science, and so on) or the prescribed units within those disciplines (Colonial Times, Our Community, Matter and Energy, Communication) but also the following:

1) Other subject disciplines: psychology, sociology, anthropology, philosophy, education
2) Media: films, books, pictures, field trips
3) Classroom situations: incidents, episodes, problems
4) Out-of-school experiences
5) The children themselves

The selection of content vehicles should be based on their

potential for helping the children to grasp the organizing ideas and achieve the desired outcomes, not on the way in which content itself is taught. Content vehicles should also be closely related to the learner's reality—his experiences and inner feelings. The teacher must assess the content the children themselves bring to school.

We distinguish three types of learners' content, in addition to the strictly cognitive material they have learned before from academic disciplines. One is experience related to persistent concerns as a growing person—concerns with identity, with power and powerlessness, with belonging and connection.

A second type of content—like the first, affective—includes the learner's feelings about his experiences related to his major underlying concerns (for example, feelings about certain television programs, friends, homework, sports).

The third area of the learner's own content is what he has learned from the social context in which he lives—his "experiential content." This is cognitive and may or may not be related to the affective content. For example, the student may have learned how to take care of his younger brothers or sisters or how to use the streets as a playground. He may know how a leader in his group must act. He may be familiar with the latest popular songs, the "in" language, and events in his neighborhood. A migrant child may have learned the characteristics of a good worker and a good foreman and how to pick the most strawberries with the least effort.

All three areas of content should be used at every step in the teaching process, along with additional content that can stimulate the learner, draw him out, and introduce new ideas to help him tap the organizing concepts.

In addition to learning as much as possible about the learner's own content, the teacher must explore existing disciplines for their potential in yielding content vehicles that relate to organizing concepts and lead to the predetermined outcomes. How, for example, does history tell a person who he is? How can science and math help students to make more accurate judgments about themselves?

Once content vehicles are selected, the teacher must translate them into lessons or units, or at least into an outline. From this point on, the teacher must also begin to outline the actual procedures and activities in which he wants the *pupils* to engage, the skills they may have to employ, and the teacher's own procedures.

LEARNING SKILLS

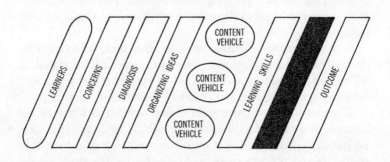

What skills will the learner need in order to work with the selected concepts and content vehicles so as to attain the desired outcomes? The model associates materials, ideas, and information with two or possibly three major learning skills that children need in order to deal with content vehicles.

The first skills area consists of what are usually called "basic skills" or tools: reading, writing, oral communication, and computation. This category should be limited to those skills that the child needs most in order to employ content vehicles. At this stage the teacher uses diagnostic procedures to measure the learner's basic skills, such as informal reading inventories and standardized tests, and his cognitive deficits, if any. These inventories help the teacher in his effort to expand the learner's resources for progressing along the path of concepts, procedures, and outcomes.

The second set consists of the skills involved in "learning to learn"—the general procedures children should know in order to become more adept at learning, at using content vehicles effectively, and at dealing with the problems that are the source of clues to concerns. These procedures include analyzing a problem and identifying its causes, learning how to deal with someone who has a different point of view, devising and trying out alternatives to a situation, and evaluating the results. Included under the "learning-to-learn" skills are the processes and ways of thinking, examining, or behaving commonly described as critical thinking, analytic procedures, discussion procedures, rational processes, inquiry, evaluating, problem solving, hypothesizing, planning, predicting outcomes, and generating alternatives. Educational researchers in Norwalk, Connecticut, for example, use the following terms for such skills: inductive and deductive reasoning, approximation, classification, transformation, analogy, comparison.[11] As in the inventory of basic skills, teachers should gather information about students in the area of process skills.

It should be emphasized that, even in terms of this model, these process skills are means to an outcome, not an end in themselves. Children need more than a well-developed faculty for critical thinking. "One does not learn to think critically by thinking critical thoughts about nothing in particular."[12] Critical thinking and other process skills clearly are important for the learner, chiefly in helping him to handle his concerns, not for extrinsic uses, such has analyzing the causes of a war or classifying rocks or insects.

The model posits a third level of skills as those used for purposes related to the self. These "self and other awareness skills" are used in recognizing and describing oneself and others multidimensionally, especially in terms of feeling; they help the learner develop a greater range of intensity and effectiveness in communicating emotional states; they tap and

[11] Dr. Esin Kaya et al., "Norwalk's Interim Report on the Behavioral Outcomes Research Study Project for Developing a Model of Educational Practices for the Elementary School," Norwalk, Conn. (Jan. 1967), p. 2.
[12] Helen McCracken Carpenter (ed.), "Skill Development in Social Studies," Thirty-Third Yearbook of the National Council for Social Studies, Washington, D.C. (1963), p. 32.

free the flow of inner feelings; they encourage candor, authenticity, and awareness of self.

Observation of a number of classroom experiences revealed that awareness skills were frequently the least developed. Children often have difficulty in expressing their feelings. A child who says that he feels nervous or happy may be unable to describe how it feels to be nervous or happy, much less *why* he feels so or whether others feel that way. If a child is asked to describe himself or someone else, he generally tells only what he or the other person looks like, where he lives, or what his activities are. Seldom does he describe himself or others in terms of feelings or thoughts.

At this as at the other levels, the teacher must establish a developmental sequence of awareness skills, in order to help children elaborate the feelings of self and others. Such a sequence might be skills that make it possible for the child to

—Recognize and describe what is happening to him, especially in terms of feeling and behavior.

—Understand how others see and describe what is happening to them.

—Compare his feeling and behavior responses with those of others.

—Analyze the varied responses and their consequences.

—Test alternatives—see how he feels when experimenting with new feelings and behaviors (for example, trying out others' feelings and behaviors).

—Make decisions—choose among the feelings and behavioral responses one has tested.

The acquisition of a good many procedural and awareness skills depends greatly on the degree to which learners can utilize basic skills, especially language. Pupils can hardly express their feelings or analyze their own and others' experiences without developing *at the same time* more elaborate speaking, listening, reading, and, perhaps, writing skills. But such skills do not have to be developed elaborately before the child begins to work with the content vehicle. They may be developed during the process or may evolve more naturally as a result of a teaching process that focuses on content relevant to feelings and concerns.

Educators using this model may find it helpful to apply any efficient and relevant means emerging from the efforts of curriculum specialists to improve, refine, and restructure the teaching of basic skills. This is not to suggest, however, that all skill development could or should be connected with all the components of this model. For our immediate purposes, skills and learning processes should be selected on the basis of their relevance to the stages of diagnosis and development of organizing ideas. Skills and processes not relevant to the model should be handled in other parts of the program.

TEACHING PROCEDURES

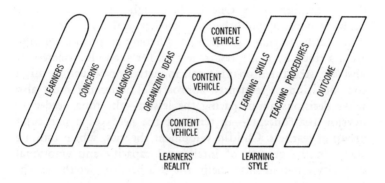

What teaching procedures, strategies, or methods are most appropriate for developing the learners' skills, content vehicles, organizing ideas, and desired outcomes? To answer this question, one should consider the methods, strategies, and all the interacting procedures the teacher utilizes in his attempt to integrate concerns, organizers, and content vehicles—in other words, *how* he uses content vehicles to link the children to organizing ideas which should affect the way they deal with their concerns.

This overall strategy offers two principal bases for selection of teaching procedures: (1) close matching of procedures with the learning styles of a particular group of students; and (2) selection of procedures that will have the most effective *affective* results.

Learning Style

When selecting teaching procedures, one should consider the way in which the child has been taught in the past and the way in which he learns best.[13] If a group of students learns best in a concrete, inductive style with a long warm-up period, their teacher would be ill-advised to use an abstract, deductive procedure of teaching.

There are at least three bases on which to ascertain children's learning style. One is the insights provided by the growing body of published work in general learning theory. The specific learning patterns of different groups of children are described by many researchers as, for example, concrete or abstract, structured or informal, inductive or deductive, direct confrontation or sequenced approach. The teacher must also make decisions about pacing the lesson—the time needed to develop the concepts—in terms of the needs of a particular group of learners. Child-development theories, which indicate stages in the growth of intellectual capacity and emotional maturity, should also help the teacher to determine the learning style most appropriate for children at certain ages. Although we believe that a child at any age can learn to be more accurate in judging himself, knowledge of child development should improve the teacher's selection of appropriate content vehicles and procedures.

[13] D. P. Ausubel, Martin Deutsch, Basil Bernstein, and Frank Riessman, to name only a few, have described learning patterns of the low-income, minority-group child. The annotated bibliography on Educational and Cultural Deprivation in B. S. Bloom, Allison Davis, and Robert Hess, *Compensatory Education for Cultural Deprivation* (New York: Holt, Rinehart & Winston, 1965), lists other significant researchers in this area.

Procedures and Affective Results

Teaching procedures that are determined only on the basis of the children's learning style may not lead to the desired outcomes. They may, in fact, defeat the purpose. For example, if the desired outcome is for learners to feel greater power, a teaching procedure that consigns them to dependent learning roles would be counterproductive. An appropriate strategy for such an outcome involves teaching procedures that provide for actual experience with power, including its responsibilities and problems, not just talk about power. In short, procedures should be consonant with content so that the procedures themselves become part of the content. This is what is meant by selecting procedures that yield *affective* results.

Some excellent examples of teaching procedures that allow the learners to experiment with power roles have been recorded. Cross-age teaching—giving older children the responsibility of teaching younger pupils—is one procedure that uses a power experience as a staging point for instruction. To strengthen learners' feelings of connection with the classroom, the teacher might have the children openly discuss individual members of the class, focusing only on their positive characteristics. To help learners become more aware of how they define themselves, the teacher could have them pretend that they had awakened that day with amnesia and ask them to reconstruct the first half hour of their morning to discover "who they are." What objects did their room contain, for example, and what was said to them by the other people in their family that could help them to establish their identity? This procedure can indicate to the teacher what children are using as criteria for self-evaluation and thus can serve as a diagnostic tool.

Whatever the procedures selected, teachers should develop interaction systems that support the learner emotionally and strengthen his feelings of self-worth. Needless to say, teacher training and efforts to change teachers' attitudes toward the learner so that a climate of mutual respect pervades the classroom should be placed in this broader personality context. Giving a teacher this new task might change his attitude more effectively than merely exhorting him to change.

EVALUATION

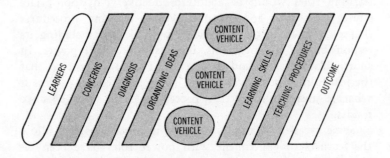

Evaluation should be a continuous process, not just a concluding step. The teacher should attempt periodically to determine the extent to which the desired outcomes are being attained and to identify strengths and weaknesses in diagnosis, content, and procedure. The effectiveness of evaluation will depend to a great extent on the accuracy with which the teacher described the learner's behavior and diagnosed his concerns at the beginning of the process. Typical evaluation questions would be: Has the children's behavior changed? Were the content vehicles the best that could have been employed? Were the cognitive skills and teacher procedures the most effective for achieving the affective goals? The questions posed during the evaluation should lead the teacher through the model again, with increasing complexity and elaboration. In other words, the model should help to uncover new learner's problems and indicate new areas to explore.

Evaluation should also suggest new procedures or content. The extent of changes in the student's assessment of reality, learning style, and learning readiness should be measured. Teachers should determine how much more deeply they want learners to deal with their concerns, and they should reassess the amount of time they now need to spend on each phase of the model.

RELATING SAMPLE LESSONS TO THE MODEL

Let us now examine two brief sample lessons in terms of the totality of the model. These lessons took place before the model was fully developed and they have shortcomings, but they do contain many elements related to the model and seemed significant to the field staff. Had the model been available at the time these lessons were taught, the teachers might have found it useful for evaluating and reconstructing their teaching practices.

A Social Studies Unit on Revolution

The following lesson took place in a fifth-grade class in Hawaii: [14]

TEACHER: Your regular teacher had to leave so for now I'm your teacher. Everyone with blue eyes please raise his hand. OK, blue-eyed people leave the class circle and go to the far corner of the room. Hurry up. Check to be sure everyone with blue eyes is out of the circle and over in the corner. Make sure. Is everyone checking? OK.

Now, blue-eyed people, when you leave the room, leave by the back door. Do not use any other door. Do you get that? The rest of us will be checking.

[At this point, the children, who until now had thought this was a game, began to challenge, but the teacher continued without permitting them to voice opinions.]

TEACHER: Blue-eyed people, keep back to the corner. When you go out, use only the drinking fountain at the end

[14] Reported by Dr. Melvin Ezer, Professor and Chairman of Elementary Education, University of Bridgeport, Bridgeport, Conn.

of the hall, and when you get on the bus, sit at the back of the bus. Eat your lunch at the back table of the dining room. OK, now, let's the rest of us get on with spelling—open your book to . . .

Blue eyes, keep quiet.

CLASS: (*paraphrased*) You can't do this to us!

TEACHER: Well, tell the principal. I told you I am taking over this class. I am running this class now.

PUPIL: But you can't do this to us. You are unfair. You can't treat them like that just because they've got blue eyes. I'll tell my father.

TEACHER: What are you kids doing? Are you protesting?

CLASS: We sure are.

At this point, the teacher drew from the class the reasons for their protest with questions such as: What does it mean to be treated unfairly or unjustly? How do you know when you're being treated unjustly? Do you always protest when you're not treated the same as everyone else? Why not? Why do people protest sometimes and not at other times? What are some of the different ways in which people protest?

The children now had a grasp of the nature of protest in terms of their own experience. The teacher then led them in a discussion of the protests of others: How can protest be recognized? How is social protest like and unlike their individual protests? During this discussion, the teacher provided most of the examples, or content, while the class analyzed, compared, and contrasted these examples with their own experiences. Students could now recognize and give examples of different manifestations of protest, both social and individual, and could make inferences about the probable causes of particular protests.

In relation to the model, the teacher started at the point of organizing ideas and proceeded through the phases of content vehicles, learning skills, and teaching procedures. His general organizing idea was "concepts related to protest and revolution." The selection of this organizing element had less to do with the manifest concerns of his pupils, however, than with what the teacher felt the children should understand.

His content vehicle was the learners themselves, and this was one of the strongest features of the lesson. The teaching procedures were primarily discussion and role-playing, which probably matched the learners' style. The learning skills (or pupil procedures) were aimed at analysis, inferences, and generalizations; there is no report of whether any specific basic skills were involved. The outcomes at which the lesson was pointed seemed to involve cognitive understanding rather than specific behavior. The learners were apparently enabled to recognize, define, characterize, and discuss protest, and they certainly felt what it was like to protest, but how these outcomes affected their subsequent behavior and their relation to protest is unclear.

The lesson is well designed from the perspective of new curricular developments, bearing out Bruner's contention that "any subject can be taught effectively in some intellectually honest form to any child at any stage of development." [15] But the sample also poses a question raised earlier: Given the learners' capability of mastering any subject that is taught appropriately, how does the teacher choose particular ideas or subjects at particular times? To some extent choice is determined by the teacher's own knowledge and ability. But we believe that the chief determinant should be the children's basic concerns—especially when the pupils come from backgrounds where knowledge for knowledge's sake is little valued (and this is by no means limited to the "disadvantaged"). The teacher must ask this question: "Why teach this material to this group of children at this time?" The lesson described above bears no evidence that this question was fully explored by the teacher.

Teaching Toward Strengthened Self-Image

A second lesson, taught to a predominantly nonwhite fifth grade in New York City,[16] significantly influenced the development and refinement of the model. The class was the

---

[15] *The Process of Education, op. cit.,* p. 33.
[16] Reported by Mrs. Luci Burrows, Educational Resources Center, Bank Street College of Education, New York, N.Y.

slowest group in its grade, and many of the students thought of themselves as failures. They very often called themselves and each other "stupid" or "dumb." Since the teacher was convinced that the students had learning potential that was being blocked by their negative view of themselves, she planned learning activities dealing directly with self-image.

A Polaroid photograph of each child was taken, in a pose that the child himself decided on—at his desk, at the teacher's desk, beside the bulletin board, at the chalkboard, or with a small prop from the classroom. The children then spent some time sharing and discussing their pictures. They began to see each member of the class was "someone special." They decided to put all their pictures in a booklet and to write essays and poems to accompany them on the subject "I Am Special." The finished booklet was then shown and read with pride to others in the school and the neighborhood.

In making her decisions, the teacher asked such questions as

    —What do my children know about themselves?
    —Is their knowledge accurate?
    —If it is not, is that fact blocking their development?
    —What do they need to know instead?
    —How can inaccurate knowledge be changed to this needed knowledge?

In terms of the model, the teacher first made a close and effective examination of the learning group to diagnose their concerns. With this knowledge and the desired new behavior in mind, she chose content vehicles and teaching procedures that were meaningful to the students. The main content of the lesson was the children themselves—a forced self-examination. The teaching procedure was structured and non-autocratic, allowing the children to bring their own specialized knowledge, since they were specialists with regard to themselves and each other, to the learning setting. Learning was concrete and active. Photographing, discussion of each picture, and writing about themselves were attempts to develop awareness skills. Most relevant components of the model—concerns, learner content, and learner-matched teaching procedures—were used, and the sequence of teaching decisions outlined earlier was followed.

The weaknesses in the lesson included the lack of a specific design for basic skill development (writing, in particular), although that was only a small part of the teacher's total program. Also, the teacher failed to define an organizing idea clearly, although one could be inferred ex post facto. But without a defined organizing element, it is unlikely that a good practice can be sustained long enough after the lesson to have any particular impact on the learner's life.

SOME UNANSWERED QUESTIONS

A few observations on step-by-step implementation of the model should be made.

Although the staff believes that the model can be useful to teachers as is, it may be more expedient to divide responsibility for the parts. Diagnosis of the learners, for example, might best be done by having a team of sociologists and psychologists observe in the classroom. They might then be able to assist the teacher in selecting concepts that could lead most readily to the desired outcomes.

It may not be essential to follow the suggested sequence for all parts of the strategy. Since there is a tendency (often observed by the staff) for teachers to spend too much time searching for and recording clues, it may be more expedient to move ahead and intuitively select organizing ideas and content that seem to relate to concerns. Once they have been developed, the teacher should check them against the clues and the over-all model. Thus, although we suggest beginning with the learner and the diagnosis of his concerns, it may be possible to develop concepts that will help learners to cope with their concerns before describing the *specific* desired outcomes. Also, several tentative content vehicles could be selected before the teacher actually pinpoints the concept common to them all.

In short, the model should serve as a flexible instrument

for stimulating the teacher's thought and analysis. If he works best at first in an intermediate section of the model, it is better that he begin there and backtrack to fill in analytical details than become blocked on earlier stages. So long as the teacher works within the framework of the total model, it does not matter whether he devises his teaching strategy by flashes of insight and sudden syntheses or by systematically pursuing the various stages of the model.

Every attempt at problem-solving generates new problems, and the development of this model has been no exception. The questions that we and others must explore in different kinds of schools with different kinds of learners and teachers include

—How do we know when a clue is related to a concern?

—What criteria, if any, should be used in establishing desired outcomes?

—How can the model avoid dealing with only negative clues?

—What cognitive skills are most appropriate for achieving affective goals?

—How can we identify learning style more specifically?

—What additional content vehicles might be developed?

—What features of a school's organization help or block a learner in working with his concerns?

—What are the most effective sequences and processes by which teachers can work on the components of the model?

—What skills and training do teachers need in order to generate practices from concerns of the youngsters?

—What manifestations of concerns normally occur at various age levels?

—What adjustments (for example, choice of appropriate content vehicles and procedures) must be made at various age levels in leading children to examine their concerns?

—What existing materials and practices complement various components of the model?

—What are identifiable starting points from which effective practices and relevant curriculum can be generated?

—In order for a person to "understand himself," what

is it that he has to understand? What is the specific *content* of that understanding?

At the time of this writing, the staff had been able to investigate only a few of these matters, essentially those involving experiments with sample materials, procedures, and new content vehicles. Chapters IV through VII deal more specifically with practice, giving examples of content and procedures that have been derived from the model.

4

IDENTITY EDUCATION

A basic goal of identity training is to help the child to recognize that his self-concept, his image of himself, is part of a network of evaluation and self-judgment to which his feelings and responses are very much related. Therefore, it seemed to us that identity education should begin with teaching the child to recognize how he judges himself, what the consequences of his judgment are, where he learned the criteria he uses for self-judgment, and what alternatives to self-judgment are available to him. The underlying assumptions were that all children are concerned with arriving at and maintaining a satisfying self-concept, and that an understanding of the elements of self-judgment would help them to do so.

With this in mind, we sought, with the help of the model, to move into the following cycle:

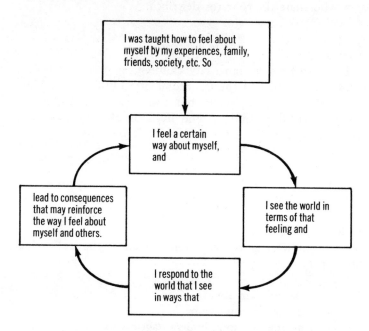

Four different strategies were employed to implement the model. The first inquired, "Who Are You and Why Are You Special?" The second used "One-Way Glasses," the third was an experiment with "Them and Us," and the fourth used chairs to illustrate the concept of subselves.

"WHO ARE YOU AND WHY ARE YOU SPECIAL?"

The following lesson series outline, prepared by Robert J. Lesniak, formerly of the Urban Teacher Preparation Program at Syracuse University, was one of the first the field staff received after early versions of the model had been distributed. Compared to subsequent outlines and actual lessons, it is a rudimentary application of the model. It is included, however, for historical interest and to indicate how a rough classroom unit plan can be generated quickly from the model. Mr. Lesniak believes that it can be used with all children who share the concerns described.

The Learners

The learners were inner-city children, aged seven to nine, whose families had an annual income of $3,000 or less. Most of the children were Negro, but there was a sprinkling of white and Indian children who lived on the fringes of the Negro ghetto.

Concerns

The children's major concerns, identified through observation, centered on self-rejection, disconnectedness, and powerlessness.

Clues indicating self-rejection included the following statements.

—"The kids are always calling me a black monkey."
—"I do not like my name."
—"I'm one of those disadvantaged kids."
—"I can't do this work. That's why I'm in this slow class."
—"I wish I were a man."

Clues indicating disconnectedness, reflecting the children's concern for connection with one another or with society at large, included

"You can't trust nobody, white or Negro."
"I'm not really accepted by white people because of my color or by Negroes because I think different than they do."

Clues indicating powerlessness, the children's concern for greater control over their destiny, included

"It's no use trying, there's nothing you can do."

"The principal runs the school and the student council, and he doesn't want to know what our problems are."

"So what if I get an education? That doesn't mean I can get a job."

Behavioral Outcomes

The primary aim of this unit was to help students to develop a more positive self-concept; the other two concerns were touched on only tangentially. The behavioral objective, therefore, was to help each child to

1) realize that his personality is a composite of many kinds of behavior, and that these behaviors are determined;
2) identify at least two ways in which he is special, citing his own special characteristics;
3) discover and remark upon the universality of his feelings;
4) analyze his likes and dislikes and compare them with the likes and dislikes of his peers.

Organizers

The following organizers served to integrate concerns, desired outcomes, and teaching procedures.

1) Everyone is very special.
2) There are many subselves that make up the self.
3) Everyone has feelings that are distinctly his own, but there are many situations in which people share the same feelings.

Content Vehicles and Teaching Procedures

Two major content vehicles were employed. The first was the book *Who Are You?*, by Joan and Roger Bradfield,[1]

[1] Racine, Wisc.: Whitman, 1966.

which the teacher read aloud in its entirety at the beginning of the unit. The second was a personal folder which each of the students constructed and contributed to in the course of the unit.

EPISODES 1 AND 2. The purpose of these "episodes" was to show some of the ways in which children differ from one another. The teacher read the book aloud and then engaged the students in discussion. His first questions related to physical characteristics.

> TEACHER:—What makes you special among everyone else in the room? Are you different in size, looks, and so on? [*He used the categories presented in the book.*]
> —What kinds of things do you like? Why?
> —What kinds of people do you like? Why?
> —What are these people like?
> —What people are important to you?
> —To whom are you important?

The teacher then asked each student to draw a self-portrait showing that he was different from everyone else. He suggested that the picture show something special about the student himself or something that he liked or did. The children added explanatory comments to their drawings. A photograph of each child was placed in his folder, facing the drawing.

EPISODE 3. The purpose of this episode was to make the children aware of their feelings.

> TEACHER:—What kinds of things make us happy? Why?
> —Can some things make us happy sometimes and sad at other times? What kind of things?
> —What people make us happy? Do they make us happy all the time?
> —Are there times when we can change things that make us happy or sad? How?

—Let's draw a picture of something that makes us happy.

—Let's write a sentence about something that makes us happy.

The completed booklets were shown to other classes, to the principal, and, most important of all, to parents, who were invited to come to the school to see them. The teacher pointed out that the booklet could be thought of as analogous to the person, or "big me," which depends on and is made up of many parts—the "little me's." Subsequent lessons were used to reinforce the concept of "me."

Learning Skills

Some basic skills were needed for working with the concepts and content vehicles pointing to the desired outcome: the ability to write a complete thought, and the ability to listen to, and take part in, discussion. They were practiced before introducing the lessons.

Learning-to-learn skills, on the other hand, were developed during the lessons themselves. The ability to generate alternative solutions is one such skill. When the teacher asked such questions as, "Are there times when we can change things that make us happy or sad?" he was furnishing practice in this skill. The ability to negotiate with people who have different points of view is another learning-to-learn skill. Role-playing provided an opportunity to develop this skill.

"ONE-WAY GLASSES"

This unit, developed by Gerald Weinstein, began with the idea that people's dominant feelings affect what they see and how they respond, and that their perception of the world is not necessarily true or shared by others. The use of "one-way glasses" emerged as a potential strategy for helping children to realize how much of the world they create through their own perceptions and the ultimate effect that their perceptions have on their response to the world and their view of themselves.

Although the strategy was conceived with no particular population of children in mind, when the experimenters moved into a classroom it took on the unique dimensions of that setting. The focus was on the problem of connectedness among the group as a whole rather than on the individual student's sense of identity. Although the experimenters had planned eventually to deal with the students' feelings about themselves and with how these feelings were learned, the time limitations imposed by the circumstance that this was a "borrowed" class did not allow them to go into these two aspects of the cycle in detail.

The Learners

The learners were thirty 10- and 11-year-olds in an ungraded demonstration school on the campus of a large, northeastern, urban university. Most of them were highly articulate strivers, capable of working well in small groups or individually on special projects. Several were quite conversant with current world problems and social issues. All seemed aware of the fact that their school was "special" and that they were not like "street kids" (their phrase) who went to nearby public schools.

Their parents were faculty members of the university or graduate or undergraduate students. It was obvious that all the children were from upwardly mobile families, although their family incomes may have been low at the time.

Only one child in the class was nonwhite. Several children had come from or lived in other countries, including Turkey, South Africa, Jamaica, Portugal, and other parts of Europe. Many had attended schools in other states before coming to the university school.

The children's interests and abilities seemed to be consistent with the school's purposes; they enjoyed and were involved in doing the things that they were expected to do at school, such as writing, discussing, and reading. Their families strongly supported and enriched their school activities. School life and home life were complementary and harmonious, since the same values, skills, and attitudes were rewarded in both places.

Concerns and Diagnosis

Most of the students indicated a concern for a positive self-image. "To be somebody, you have to make the rest of the kids look up to you" was a widely held sentiment. One child said, "You have to be independent and not do what everyone else is doing." Another said, "To stand out I take the opposite side of every issue—I'm very individualistic."

A concern for power or some kind of control over people and events seemed pervasive. "In this class you have to be a controller—cool and tough—and be able to take control of any group and run it" was a typical attitude. "You have to fight, squabble, gossip your way to the top." "You have to be secluded and not get involved unless you can be in control." Teachers who curtailed control were resented: "He's always making me do things when I don't want to."

The verbal cues of the children in this classroom seemed to indicate that their two major concerns were in the areas of self-concept and power. Most of them manifested both concerns by competing to make the cleverest, brightest remarks, not only to attract the attention of teachers and classmates but also to "put down" other children in a kind of one-upmanship game. The more verbally competent they were, the more eagerly they responded to any challenge or new learning situation, in part because they expected to be, and usually were, successful.

The determining factor in favor of participation rather than withdrawal seemed to be, not intelligence but, rather, a sense of potency and self-importance. Most of those who sought to monopolize the floor seemed confident that their influence would eventually prevail. Some of them, however, seemed to talk compulsively in an effort to maintain their identity and power.

But the children who withdrew altogether were perhaps

least sure of their identity or of the potency of their ideas. They manifested the two concerns by withholding their opinions for fear of being ridiculed. Unsure of their ability to make a contribution or even to draw an audience, they said nothing. Many withdrew entirely, perhaps hoping in this manner to preserve some sort of identity and power.

Both the participating and the withdrawing students showed their concern for identity. When asked what were the "easiest" glasses to wear when regarding the world, most replied "suspicious." This choice reflected an underlying fear of being exposed, deprecated, made to feel worthless, small, or helpless. Articulated suspiciousness often indicated a basic fear: "Are they going to make fun of me?" "Will they flunk me?" "Are they laughing at *me?*" The children's suspicious outlook served as a form of self-protection. The same concern was also apparent in frequently expressed wishes to be looked up to, to be an individual, to be different.

Some members of the class expressed concern for self-identity by assuming grandiose appellations. One boy frequently reminded his classmates that he was "God" and wished to be addressed as such. His manner was humorous, but even sarcastically tendered acquiescence elicited his manifest delight. At first glance this might have appeared to be an individual idiosyncracy, but closer attention revealed it to be fairly common behavior. A second student habitually described himself as "fabulous," and a third, named Andrew, liked to call himself "St. Andrew." Even the unflattering sobriquet "the spy" seemed to achieve a welcome fixed role identity for one rather withdrawn child.

Generally, it was difficult to distinguish the group's concern for power from its concern for self-identity, since the two concerns were usually intertwined. Many disparaging references seemed to have a dual function, for when one student called another "stupid" or "superior-acting," he seemed to be trying to enhance both his power and his self-identity. Sometimes, however, the children showed a clear concern for power unencumbered by any implication of concern for self-identity.

It is probable that many of these attitudes were encouraged by, or at least acceptable to, parents and teachers. Outgoing, clever, probing, and dissenting verbal behavior is generally valued in a university milieu, where it is assessed by parents, teachers, and peers as an indication of an inquisitive, intelligent mind. (This is not to say that working independently and quietly and discovering on one's own, as both the participating and the withdrawing students were apt to do, were not socially acceptable kinds of behavior.)

The children's apparent concern for power and self-identity was in no way matched by a concern for connectedness, although all signs seemed to point to a great deal of disconnectedness among them. For example, students seldom listened to what their classmates had to say; the aim of each was to be heard first, to get out what he had to say. Reactions to the contributions of other students were generally negative. As a matter of fact, the class seemed to relish disconnectedness as a way of being "against what others do," of being a "controller," of being "very individualistic," of even being "God" or "St. Andrew." Within the limited world of their classroom it made for survival, for self-identity, for power. In the eyes of some of the children, the only alternative means of maintaining some sort of self-image (but not potency) was withdrawal. Either type of behavior intensifies the disconnectedness among the students.

It was our conviction that a sense of connectedness was prerequisite for the development of stronger feelings of potency in these children. In classrooms where there is little connectedness and much competition, only a few children—the leaders—can ever gain a feeling of potency; the rest of the class feel powerless. However, even the few leaders in the class under observation did not seem to feel powerful. The tenuousness of their position, their need for connectedness, and their narrow definition of power precluded this.

We hypothesized that a connected classroom situation would encourage the development of a positive self-concept and a sure sense of power in each of the students. Given a connected environment, students would have little need to assert their own power and identity by disparaging others, and the possibilities for seeing others' strong points would be enhanced. When, in such circumstances, the children tuned in, the likelihood was that what they heard would improve their image of themselves as well.

Behavioral Outcomes

In the series of lessons described below, connectedness was the instrumentality through which the children realized their own constructive power and positive self-concepts. It was hoped that as a result of the lessons they would develop more constructive patterns of behavior for dealing with their concerns. Ideally, they would be able to verbalize their new appreciations. They would be able to say that they felt in control without being controlling; that stepping on other people was not the only way to "stay on top"; that they could see things in new ways that made it more possible for them to be themselves; that seeing more in others, they could see more in themselves; that they no longer feared loss of face as a consequence of being affirmative about others; that there were aspects of themselves that would appear admirable to others; and that grandiose labels were not necessary to bolster self-esteem. It was also to be hoped that the students' behavioral changes would lend themselves to objective verification by the teachers in charge. Such verification would be based on the answers to questions like the following:

> Do the children encourage and listen to one another's viewpoints?
> Do the children acknowledge their own and others' strong points?
> Do the withdrawn children respond more?

In general, we hoped that the children would begin to diagnose themselves and others in the classroom in terms of strategies—that, in effect, they would ask: "What strategies am I using that may limit my potency and self-identity? and "What strategies might I develop or expand to help me gain identity and power?"

Organizers

Given the concerns and diagnosis described, three major organizing ideas were selected to effect the desired outcomes. The first organizer was designed to widen horizons. The role-playing in the classroom, manifest in the widespread practice of labeling, coupled with the kind of participation or withdrawal that took place, was symptomatic of a narrow range of perception of self and others. To counter this narrow view, it seemed necessary to select a broadening organizing idea. As our first organizer, therefore, we selected the theme: *There are many ways of seeing the same situation*.

The second organizing idea was selected because it seemed that the students' perceptions of others and the world, as reflected in their comments to one another, stemmed from their own perceptions of self. We would work with this idea: *Perceptions and responses at any given time depend on the feelings and thoughts that accompany them*. This organizer was helpful in making each child more conscious of his part in creating the world he sees and his role in it. We wanted the children to be aware that their way of seeing and responding to people and events at any particular time helps to determine, in turn, who *they* are in the eyes of others and what their role is.

Finally, the major purpose of our lessons was to expand the students' repertoire of strategies for perceiving themselves and gaining identity and control. Previously the children had maintained their own identity by using others'. We wanted to see if it was possible to teach them satisfying but nondestructive strategies for relating to other people. The aim was to have each student realize that restricting himself to a single view of people and situations limited his power, identity, and relations with others, and that if he could, through practice, learn to see some situations in new ways, he might find these to be more satisfying, potent, and useful than the old. The third organizing idea seemed relevant to these ends: *Limited perception constricts the individual's view of himself as well as the world*.

We felt that these three organizers, implemented by appropriate content and procedure, would help the children to take inventory of their own perceptions, to distinguish between one person's perceptions and another's, to experiment with different ways of regarding the same things, and to explore the consequences of regarding them in fixed ways.

Content Vehicles

The children themselves were the indicated content vehicles for the experiment. No books, films, or subject disciplines were used in the lessons described below. Classroom situations, pupil experiences, and personal feelings contributed to the content. The device through which most of the content filtered was the notion of "glasses," which the participants pretended to wear or, in fact, wore.

The episodes described below were abstracted from seven lessons, each lasting from one to two hours, which took place over a period of three weeks toward the end of the school year. This is not a verbatim account, as even the language of the excerpts is condensed. But the abstracts do indicate what actually happened in the classroom and do represent the content vehicles and many of the teacher's procedures.

LESSON 1. The purpose of this lesson was to show the students (1) that there are different ways of seeing the same situation and (2) that one's state of mind or feeling influences one's perceptions—that, in effect, each person creates his own world out of his own perceptions.

A blackboard exercise introduced two role-playing games.

> TEACHER: (*drawing two vertical lines of different lengths on the blackboard*) : What do you see?
> STUDENT: Two lines. One's longer than the other.
> TEACHER: Now think of these lines as two telephone poles. What do you see?
> STUDENT: One's farther away than the other.
> TEACHER: Now try to think again of the lines as two different lengths. How many find this difficult? [*Many students indicated that they found it difficult*]

TEACHER: Now you can see that often when you have a certain idea or feeling it's difficult to see things the way you might if you did not have that idea or feeling.

The teacher now held up two pairs of sunglasses, each with a different color lenses. He explained that these were very special glasses, that each pair colored the wearer's view of the world with a particular feeling.

TEACHER: The first pair of glasses are "suspicious" glasses. When a person wears them, he regards whatever he sees or hears with suspicion. [*The teacher asked for a volunteer to put on the suspicious glasses and tell the class what he saw.*]

VOLUNTEER (*looking at two children who were talking and laughing, as he put on the glasses*): I wonder if they're talking about me. Are they laughing at me? [*The teacher asked that questions be addressed to the volunteer.*]

STUDENT: Who's your best friend?

VOLUNTEER: Why does he want to know that? Are they going to try to take my friends away?

TEACHER: (*holding up second pair of glasses*): I have a second pair of glasses, which are rose-colored. They make whoever wears them see and hear with this feeling: "No matter what anyone says to me, I know they really care for me."

[*Teacher asked for and secured the cooperation of another volunteer. Throughout the dialogue that followed the teacher sought to clarify the volunteer's responses by asking: "Are you acting suspicious or just curious?" "Do you really feel that way, or are you exaggerating your reactions?" "Do you really think they might be trying to do that to you?"*]

TEACHER: Let's get some reactions from our volunteer.

STUDENT (*to second volunteer*): You're just a noisy little pipsqueak!

VOLUNTEER 2: He always calls me a little pipsqueak,

but that shows he really notices me and probably likes smaller people like me.

STUDENT: How come you're always hanging around with Betty?

VOLUNTEER: I bet she asked that because she really wants me to try and make more friends.

In another segment, three students playing the part of mother, father, and child sat around a "breakfast table," directed by the teacher, and were joined by another student, role-playing the second child in the family, who was wearing the "suspicious" glasses. Without really involving the second child in their own conversation, various members of the family directed remarks to him. (The second child was instructed to call out "freeze" whenever he wanted to say what he was thinking.)

SECOND CHILD: Why don't they say hello? Are they mad at me?

FATHER: Pass the butter, please.

SECOND CHILD: He's gonna take all the butter, I bet.

MOTHER: How do you want your eggs?

SECOND CHILD: Scrambled, but I bet she won't give them to me. Everyone else has fried eggs.

FIRST CHILD: What are you going to do this weekend?

SECOND CHILD: Why does she want to know where I'm going this weekend? They want to follow me around. Or do they just want to get me out of the house? Or are they going to tell me I have to stay home and work?

After a few children had tried this role-play wearing "suspicious" glasses, the same situation was repeated with the second child wearing the rose-colored glasses.

SECOND CHILD:—They really understand me. They're not talking to me much because they know I don't like to talk this early in the morning.

—Mom's nice to me, she's letting me choose what kind of eggs I want.

—I bet they want me to have a good
time this weekend.

To sum up the lesson, the teacher asked the children to
make lists of the different kinds of glasses people might wear.
They proposed

show off	boasting	sissyish	nobody-loves-me
gloomy	probing	yes-y	stubborn
helpful	boyish	flirtatious	contented
scared	girlish	hateful	proud

The children were then asked to produce a list of glasses
that would have the opposite effect of the ones named above.

LESSON 2. With the same general purpose as in the first lesson, the teacher expanded the idea of the glasses and provided experiences for wearing different kinds of glasses. The
teacher asked the class to look through some of the glasses
they had listed during the previous lesson and pretend to
get the feeling ascribed to them. The teacher called on one
student after another to try on each of the following kinds
of glasses and react to them.

TEACHER: "Gloomy" glasses.
STUDENT: It's going to be a boring day, no fun. Noth-
ing much is going to happen. We're going to write today.
. . . Oh, I hate writing. It's just awful.
TEACHER: "Things-aren't-really-that-bad" glasses.
STUDENTS:—I had an awful breakfast, but it wasn't
that bad.
—I have a lot of math to do, but it really
isn't that hard.
—I have a doctor's appointment today and
he'll probably give me a shot . . . ugh. . . . But I've had
shots before and have gotten over them.
TEACHER: "Suspicious" glasses.
STUDENT: He's not gonna pass us if we don't do well
on this.

TEACHER: "Curious" glasses.

STUDENT: Gee, I wonder what Mr. _____'s first name is. I wonder what we'll be doing today.

The teacher now asked the students to define the meaning of each pair of glasses as clearly as they could and to distinguish sharply between the effects of one pair and another.

Then the teacher asked the class to respond in two or three written sentences to a series of situations, comments, and people as seen through each of the four pairs of glasses discussed above: gloomy, things-aren't-really-that-bad, suspicious, and curious. The teacher described a hypothetical situation:

"Your parents have an out-of-town couple as guests for the weekend. The woman is an old friend of your mother. She and her husband are going to tour the city on Saturday afternoon. They'll probably go sightseeing, shopping, maybe to a park or museum. They ask if you'd like to come along, and your mother says, 'Yes, why don't you go with them?' "

STUDENT (*looking through gloomy glasses*): They'll probably baby me. I'll die of boredom. I've been to all those old museums.

The students were then asked to react to a surprise summons to the school office, to a hippie, to the mayor, to a television star, and to several photographs showing people interacting in various ways. Reactions were read aloud and compared. Some children had trouble adjusting to particular glasses, and the teacher explored this with the class:

TEACHER:—Suppose a person finds it hard to wear a certain pair of glasses—what does that mean?
—Is it hard to write about the kinds of glasses you hardly ever wear? Or is it the other way around—harder to write about the glasses you usually wear?

LESSON 3. The purpose of this lesson was to help the students better differentiate the glasses they have discussed, see that many people have a fixed perception of others, and examine the consequences of the "one-way" behavior that ensues.

The teacher distributed copies of two categories charts. He asked the students to use Categories Chart I to conjure up the idea of a prominent person by naming the animal, food, car, and music that the person would call to mind if he were

Categories Chart I: President Johnson

Observer's Glasses	Animal	Food	Car	Music
Curious	Cat—He pries into things.	Chinese food	Hopped-up racing car —you inquire about it.	Slow, or stop and start with contrast
Things-aren't-really that-bad	Eagle	Apples	Lincoln Continental	Jazz
Suspicious	Panther or cougar	Fried eggs— They bubble and pop. You can't tell when he'll do something	Black sedan	Scary
Gloomy	Rhino (stubborn)	Southern fried chicken	Black sedan on the go from the cops	"Devilish" or "sinful"

observed through the glasses indicated on the chart. The children were then asked to write a few sentences justifying their choices. One child explained his choice of the weasel as the animal that would remind him of President Lyndon B. Johnson if he were wearing "suspicious" glasses by saying, "President Johnson is a weasel because he is always doing things so fast that we can't follow."

Categories Chart II required students to derive a descrip-

Categories Chart II: My Teacher

Observer's Glasses	Animal	Color	Sound	Building
Curious	Dog—Always poking around	Green—Always asking questions	Flute—Sweet, and he makes us do things	Odd-looking
Things-aren't-really-that-bad	Cat—Sometimes purring, sometimes clawing	Blue—Nice and fierce	Violin—Soft and loud	It has good things and bad
Suspicious	Fox—Always slyly making us work	Red—Always acting suspicious	Rock and roll—Always bursts into something new	Skyscraper—Always going far into things
Gloomy	Mule—He is always stubborn about things	Black—Always making me do math	Endless drum—Always nagging	Haunted house—Always springs surprises, like work

tion based on the animal, color, sounds, and building that would be called to mind by a prominent person, classmate, teacher, or friend when seen through the indicated glasses. Some children had more difficulty than others in fulfilling the assignment. The students read and commented on each other's work. "Gloomy music is gloomy music," one student exclaimed. "When you're wearing gloomy glasses, everyone looks gloomy in the same way, so you pick the same music or food for everyone."

The teacher seized on the remark for further exploration.

TEACHER:—Is it true that when you wear your gloomy glasses you usually pick the same gloomy music, regardless of whom you're describing? Did you have trouble finding

a type of gloomy (curious, suspicious, and so on) music
(color, animal, and so on) for President Johnson that is
different from the gloomy music you pick for your
teacher?

—When you're wearing any particular pair
of glasses, is it hard to see the actual characteristics of an
individual?

— Does wearing one pair of glasses most of
the time limit the kinds of things you see about others? the
world? yourself?

A brief discussion followed.

LESSON 4. The purpose set forth for Lesson 3 was enlarged
on here. The teacher introduced the notion of behavioral one-
wayness by calling attention to this quality in a number of
comic book and television characters who act the same way
all the time: brave, good, bad, and so on.

TEACHER: Have you ever seen Batman do anything
bad?

The teacher asked for a volunteer to play the role of Batman in order to help figure out what kind of glasses he wore.
Several students who were familiar with the Batman television series volunteered to act as interviewers.

STUDENT:—What do you believe in, Batman?

—I'm a criminal, Batman. What is my problem?

As a result of the role-playing activity, the students
labeled Batman's glasses "self-righteous." The remainder of
the lesson dwelt on the meaning and implications of the label.
This was especially important since only a few members of
the class understood the term initially.

In another role-playing activity, a student was sent out
of the room "for talking," and "counselors" talked with
him.

SELF-RIGHTEOUS COUNSELOR: Why were you sent

out? For talking? You shouldn't talk in class. It's not right. You won't learn anything that way.

UNSELF-RIGHTEOUS COUNSELOR: When I was a kid I talked, too, but you don't learn as much as you could if you weren't talking.

A student was caught stealing something from a candy store.

SELF-RIGHTEOUS COUNSELOR: It isn't right to steal. Your parents must have told you never to seal. You should listen to them.

UNSELF-RIGHTEOUS COUNSELOR: You stole because your friends do it. Well, maybe you shouldn't do everything your friends do.

Using both situations, the class studied the differences between the self-righteous and unself-righteous counselors. For reinforcement, the class was asked for further examples of television personalities or characters in books or cartoons who wear one-way glasses. Charlie Brown, Lucy, and Matt Dillon were given as examples.

The teacher now set up a role-playing situation involving five people, all wearing different kinds of glasses: self-righteous, curious, everything-will-turn-out-all-right, suspicious, and impatient. They all attended a "planning meeting" to select one television show about which all five participants would report to the class. The teacher assigned each role-player a coach who sat behind him and fed him ideas or comments to assist him in the dialogue. A discussion of the role-playing followed:

TEACHER: What happens in a meeting when each person wears a different pair of one-way glasses? Have you found that this happens in real situations?

The lesson was reinforced with a homework assignment. Volunteers were asked to write a ten-minute script dealing with any of the role-playing situations. The dialogue, they were told, was not to be phony or obvious but was to reflect clearly the kinds of glasses that were worn. Other students were asked to watch television and report to the class about the types of glasses the television characters were "wearing."

LESSON 5. The purpose of this lesson was to help the children perceive the difficulties in developing new views of other people.

The session opened with a discussion of the homework assignment which required the students to identify the glasses worn by whichever television characters they had watched.

TEACHER: Do the characters wear these glasses all the time? Describe the situations in which they wear these glasses.

Turning to a new activity, the teacher selected two students to role-play interviewers assigned to question the teacher about his choice of profession. Unknown to the rest of the class, the role-playing interviewers had been instructed to wear different pairs of glasses, one "curious," the other, "put-down" glasses.

CURIOUS INTERVIEWER: Why did you choose to be a teacher? What did you have to do to become one?

PUT-DOWN INTERVIEWER: How come you're in teaching? Because it's easy? Couldn't you do anything better than teach?

The teacher addressed himself to the class

TEACHER: How did each person make me feel? How did I feel about each person? What kinds of glasses might each interviewer have been wearing?

In the ensuing discussion, the students accused the put-down role-player of drawing his own conclusions. They identified him as self-righteous, suspicious, executing. The curious role-player, on the other hand, was thought to be questioning, probing, supportive—and nosy.

The teacher confided to the class how he felt with each interviewer; small and inferior with the put-down role-player; relaxed, supported, and comfortable with the curious role-player. He examined the differences between put-down, curious, and suspicious glasses with the class and asked the students to recall how they felt the last time they wore each of these glasses. A person's way or style of questioning and commenting, the teacher explained, can affect another's feelings.

Now another team repeated a similar role-playing situation. This time, however, the two role players, again wearing curious and put-down glasses, interviewed a third student rather than the teacher and were assisted by two coaches. "What are you going to do this summer (or during the next vacation)?" was the topic.

The entire class participated in the next activity. The children were instructed to wear curious glasses and were invited to play "Twenty Questions" with the teacher. They were told to ask him any question that could be answered by "yes," "no," or a short qualifying answer such as "sometimes" or "no more than anyone else." The rules of the game required him to have in mind a clear image of a very definite type of person but the only clue the teacher was supposed to give the class to his pretended identity was that he belonged to a certain category of people, such as sixth-graders, adults, or teenagers. He chose to think of himself as a sixth-grader with lots of friends who was a person of importance in his out-of-school life but did poorly in school and therefore did not feel very good about himself there. The class was supposed to discover as much of this as it could. The teacher assigned a student to write the questions and answers on the board, and then the game began. (The game can be thought of as the beginning of training in inquiry skills as applied specifically to the affective domain.)

STUDENTS:—Do you feel angry about our asking questions?

—Do you think that you could really do anything you set your mind to?

—Do you consider yourself a good worker in school?

—Do you consider yourself an absolute failure?

—Are you sure of yourself?

When there were five questions left to be asked, the teacher advised the students to consult among themselves and select what they thought would be the best questions. After the last question had been posed, the teacher asked the students what they knew about the person he had been impersonating. At last, he told them what the person was like. The class reviewed its questions and answers in the light of the disclosure.

LESSON 6. The purpose here was to explore the nature of one person who is a member of the in-group and another who is left out, while giving the class practice in formulating "curious" questions about people.

In another game of "Twenty Questions," the teacher assumed the role of a sixth-grader who had built a protective wall around himself. He had many good ideas but, having often been squelched, he found it safer to repress them than to risk derision by putting them forth. (The teacher did not tell the children that he had actually patterned the role after some of them. As the game proceeded, however, it became clear that many of them understood this to be so.)

In this second game, the teacher delegated the role of moderator to a student. It was his job to recognize speakers and clarify their questions as necessary. The moderator was instructed to be supportive and to give preference to the quieter members of the class. From time to time, he was told, he might wish, and was to feel free, to summarize what had been learned up to then about the person whose role the teacher had assumed.

When the twenty questions had been posed, the teacher disclosed his pretended identity. As in the previous lesson, the class reviewed their questions and answers in the light of the disclosure.

For the next activity, the teacher divided the class into groups of four, each of which was to select four pairs of glasses that the member thought would be most useful for "a child who was to be enrolled in the class shortly." A reporter from each group then told the class what kinds of glasses his group had selected for the newcomer, what they could be expected to accomplish for their wearer, and how he should behave while wearing them.

"*Secluded*" *glasses*: They prepare you to be blank. Try not to get involved. If possible join a secluded group as far from human thought as possible. Bring a toy to amuse yourself with in school.

"*Cool, tough*" *glasses*: They prepare you to be the best at parties. If you are not, fight, squabble, gossip your way to the top. Have lots of admirers. And put them down.

"*Studious*" *glasses*: They prepare you to stick to your studies whatever else happens. As this is a small group, make your outward appearances cool.

"*Controller's*" *glasses*: They prepare you to take control of any group and run it. You have to be a quick-change artist to do it. You must have another controller as a friend to control the room. Again, make kids look up to you. If you must, put them in the background.

"*Serious*" *glasses*: They help you not to wander onto a different subject all the time. Try not to laugh and giggle at every little thing.

"*Humorous*" *glasses*: They make you not thoroughly humorous, but able to throw in a few little jokes here and there, and not be always pessimistic.

"*Independent*" *glasses*: With them you're not sticking to the same ideas, not always changing. You're not doing what everyone else is doing and not always being the same person. Consider everything.

"Nonaggressive" glasses: With them you're not losing your temper all the time and yelling and screaming. Have patience.

The teacher discussed these choices with the class.

TEACHER: Are some of these glasses contradictory? When would be the best times to wear some of these glasses in class?

LESSON 7. In this last lesson, the purpose was to give the class practice with a set of glasses that it would be most helpful for them to wear—particularly, glasses that enabled them to seek out the most positive qualities in themselves and in others.

The class was asked to put away their put-down and suspicious glasses and to try on a pair of glasses that are very difficult to wear. Other students, he warned, and even adults, have a hard time wearing these glasses for more than a few minutes. They are "strong-point" glasses.[2]

TEACHER: Now we'll choose somebody to come to the front of the room and tell us how he sees himself through his strong-point glasses.

At the teacher's request, members of the class dropped slips of paper bearing their names into a hat, and one was drawn. The person chosen went to the front of the room.

TEACHER: How do you think this person feels?
STUDENTS: Embarrassed.
TEACHER: You can help him overcome his embarrassment by not making faces at him or making fun of him and by looking at him supportively.

[2] This situation was suggested by Herbert A. Otto, "Multiple Strength Perception Method, Minerva Experience, and Others," in *Group Methods Designed to Actualize Human Potential* (Salt Lake City: University of Utah, 1967).

The teacher warned the selected person that his strong-point glasses might occasionally slip, in which case he might don his "crack-a-joke-about-me" or put-down glasses. The group was asked to be on the lookout for such lapses. Now the teacher suggested that in the event the target person ran out of positive things to say about himself, he was to feel free to admit it and ask the class for help in finding additional strong points. The class was cautioned once again about the difficulty of its assignment. With this in mind, the teacher, too, was prepared to help students find strong points if necessary.

FIRST PERSON (*a strong, quiet, interested, class leader*) : I'm good in science and in playing baseball and all kinds of sports and at home when it comes to helping around the house. I'm strong in the classroom in writing poetry and discovering and exploring new things. I like to do a lot of reading. I think I can produce a lot of ideas and create things. I think that's all, does anyone have anything else?

STUDENTS:—You're creative.
—You as a person are nice. You're not a boaster, put-down, or suspicious. You're a good worker and compatible—not always criticizing.
—You're good at organizing, like when you were class president.
—You have a good sense of humor. You can hold up against your three brothers. You're tactful.
—You don't always try to be on top.

The strong-points situation was repeated several times, giving as many students as possible a chance to tell about their own strong points.

SECOND PERSON (*also a class leader*) : I play sports and understand them. I do a lot of exploring. I cartoon and do pretty good artwork. I try anything. I clean up.

I participate in school politics. I like most animals. I read a lot. I like photography and coin collecting.

The teacher reminded this student to talk about his strong points and not merely what he liked to do, unless he thought those things were his strong points, too.

STUDENTS:—You're sort of what I'd like to be. You can really concentrate on one thing and not worry about other things.

—You're interesting to be with.

—You type fast.

—When you get an idea, you stick to it.

THIRD PERSON (*a small, fidgety child, not in the in-group*): I like hamsters, stamps, and baseball. I like to write. I like poetry. I like all animals.

STUDENTS:—You're "big brothery" to all your brothers and sisters. You take care of them.

—You're sort of untouched by civilization. You're not conceited, you have the simple things.

—When you want to learn, you can.

—You're always there.

—You're dependable and amiable.

—You have bounce-ability.

The teacher now intervened.

TEACHER: How do you feel about this whole idea? How do you feel when this is going on? Why are these the most difficult glasses to wear? We're often taught to look at the worst in ourselves and others; to be overly critical. When we wear one-way glasses or only a few pairs of glasses—that is, critical or put-down glasses— we see only a piece of the world. The more different kinds of glasses we are able to wear, the more we are able to see.

Learning Skills

Verbal, writing, and acting skills, in most of which the students were fairly proficient, were basic to each of the lessons described. However, the experiment also required a number of learning-to-learn skills, in which the children were less adept. Group-discussion skills and procedures were the most obvious of these. No formal attempt was made to instruct the class in discussion procedures except to remind the students periodically to raise their hands when they wished to speak and to listen to others. But discussion procedures were subtly conveyed throughout, particularly during the two "Twenty Questions" lessons, which made it clear how discussion style or interviewing technique can influence attitudes. In order for the last five questions to elicit a significant response, the children had to, and did, reason together in a cooperative spirit.

Practice in the skill of making clear distinctions and classifications occurred whenever the students had to identify and describe the nature or effect of given pairs of glasses. Filling out the categories charts also contributed to the development of these skills. The ability to analyze and hypothesize was developed in the course of several episodes. Prescribing the glasses that would be most helpful to a newcomer and determining why it was difficult for some children to wear certain kinds of glasses were exercises in analyzing and hypothesizing. As a matter of fact, these skills were used and developed in the course of almost every role-playing activity.

Perhaps the most important learning-to-learn skill developed during the experiment was the ability to express feelings. The device of the glasses enabled the children to talk about their own and others' feelings instead of just cognitive matters. The strong-point glasses were especially powerful in helping the students to express feelings and thoughts about themselves and others.

Teaching Procedures

Most of the teaching procedures are self-evident in the preceding account of the episodes themselves, but it may be helpful to discuss some of them further. Throughout the series of lessons, the teacher attempted to select procedures that would yield the most *affective* results. The children were constantly propelled into role-playing situations in which they had to feel what it is like to "wear different kinds of glasses" and to interact with one another in a variety of ways. As noted, the strong-point technique described in the final episode proved especially effective in this respect. It allowed the children to discuss their positive feelings about themselves and others and gave them practice in behaving positively and supportively.

No conscious effort was made to match teaching procedures and learning styles. The teacher did, however, take advantage of the children's high verbal ability, matching the level of his discourse and abstractions to their greater-than-average facility. Although "teacher talk" never supplanted the concrete experiences furnished by the extensive application of the role-playing technique, it must be said that the verbal sophistication of this class made it relatively easy to blend the inductive and deductive methods of teaching. Similarly, the ability of this class to work independently was put to good use in the preparation of categories charts and written statements, but no deliberate effort was made to match this predominant learning style either. Any such attempt would have interfered with the accomplishment of the desired outcomes, which were overwhelmingly dependent on successful interaction.

Very early in the series of lessons, the teacher signaled his desire for openness by asking the class to be suspicious of him. "Put on your suspicious glasses and look at me," he invited, thus making it possible for any distrust of him or what he was doing to be aired in a socially acceptable way. This teacher's practice of introducing lessons with humorous anecdotes which tied in with the main purpose of the lesson contributed to the informal atmosphere.

At the outset, however, the teacher found it necessary to invoke a stopgap management technique, making it very clear that he would recognize only those students who raised their hands: "I can't hear you unless you raise your hand." "I'd like to explore what you just said, but not until you raise your hand." The desired outcomes could be approximated only if the more aggressive children were restrained and induced to listen to others.

Calling often on the low men on the totem pole—the withdrawn children, who occasionally raised their hands but were not aggressive enough to call out—served a dual purpose: It helped to reinforce the custom of hand-raising and it coaxed some of the shy children into the group. Connectedness was also fostered by the use of "coaches" during role-playing activities. This not only permitted the participation of more children than could otherwise have participated, but also encouraged many of the withdrawn students to contribute without having to perform publicly. On the other hand, enlisting the more outgoing students as coaches helped to curb their verbal aggressiveness and channeled their talents constructively. This procedure helped to develop more desirable interaction within the class.

During the strong-point episode, the teacher used the technique of reacting with the class when he moved in to uncover strong points in the target students that had been overlooked by their classmates. At such times, the teacher's example encouraged student responses and saved face for the target student as well.

Another technique was to appoint one of the more intrusive students as moderator; the "Twenty Questions" game provided the opportunity. As has been pointed out, the moderator was instructed to encourage the participation of those of his classmates who seldom contributed to discussions and to comment on the give-and-take of the others. He was forced to listen to his class-mates very carefully and with an open mind. In the episode cited, the behavior of the first moderator was exemplary

Finally, the relevance of atmosphere and attitude to the teaching procedure should be examined. The teacher handled the class candidly, supportively, and with humor. In a number of role-playing situations, he acted as a peer of the students, thus demonstrating his capacity to identify with them in a supportive way.

Evaluation

Many of the desired outcomes seemed to be achieved during the course of the experiment. As the series of lessons drew to a close, the original participants seemed more attentive to others and less destructive. Positive observations about others were expressed more freely as the students glimpsed more strong points in themselves and others. One student, for example, exclaimed admiringly to the rest of the class about a target person during the strong-points episode: "Gee, I just never thought of John that way!" Before, during, and after classes, the students frequently analyzed situations, themselves, and each other as if seeing through one or another kind of glasses. Several (but not enough) of the withdrawn students began to participate, physically moving their chairs into centers of discussion. That too few of these students learned to do this must be regarded as a shortcoming of the experiment.

In other respects, too, the desired outcomes fell short of what was hoped for. In most cases this reflected the brevity of the series: Insufficient attention had been given to specific problems. Not enough was done, for example, to investigate the consequences of limiting oneself to a single viewpoint, especially the one that the children in this class seemed to find most satisfactory. It would have been desirable for the students to have been brought to realize that with "curious glasses" one can participate without having to be right. It could also have been pointed out that "clarifying" glasses can be worn to help others in discussions while at the same time satisfying the "clarifier's" need for power. Neither of these objectives was accomplished.

Written student evaluations of the lesson series produced some interesting observations. Their new-found ability to "dope out" people intrigued some of the children, while the "pointlessness" of talking about feelings irritated others. Many students regretted the scarcity of time.

The use of actual glasses as props elicited the most comment. There was considerable difference of opinion, but most of the children favored it. One said, "Real glasses are good because they catch a person's eye and keep it." Others liked them "because they make you believe it better," or "help you really feel it." A minority of students bridled at the use of props. "Don't use the glasses idea. Use the phrase 'different kinds of feelings,'" one child suggested. Another said, "I thought the glasses idea was not very good. It made me feel like I was in a first grade or something." In retrospect, it might have been wise to discontinue using the glasses after one or two lessons, since after a certain point there was considerable horseplay whenever the actual prop glasses were donned.

Five students thought they were better able to "dope out" people at the end of the lesson series than they had been at the beginning. "Now I notice I can see through a person easier," said one. "They're good for testing out other people," wrote another, "I know now that M. is suspicious and thinking suspicious things," concluded a third. Such statements might be interpreted to mean that the students had gained a greater sense of potency or that the glasses were being used as weapons, more destructive of others than supportive to the wearers. A discussion of this very point, "Are the glasses weapons or tools?" might have sensitized these children to this kind of misuse of the glasses.

A few children made critical comments about the discussions of feelings. "Everybody has feelings anyway," wrote one especially withdrawn youngster, "so I don't see why people should try to teach people about them. What's the point of it?" His sentiment may have been shared by one or two other children who observed: "It really didn't help me a lot," or words to that effect. It can be inferred that these students failed to accept the ability to express feelings as a necessary skill or one that should be learned. It might have been advisable to probe with the class into the difficulties of talking about feelings, and whether or not such talk is desirable in the first place.

Typical comments about the shortage of time were: "I think you could have gotten to more glasses with more time" and "We should have gone over more different kinds of glasses and found uses for them." But one student wrote: "Although there are millions of kinds of glasses, these four [suspicious, curious, things-aren't-really-that-bad, and gloomy] covered almost all of them.

By and large, student reactions to the series were positive. Statements like the following were common:

I've learned how to see people in different ways and to see how other people look at us.

The glasses have helped me and other people mostly in realizing that different people do not always think the same, and it has helped me look at things as if I were another person.

It helped me to view other people's strong points and also to realize my own.

I learned about glasses that can help and glasses that can't help.

If I get to go into show biz like I would like to, this will help me to be able to change my personality. Even if I don't, it shows me different ways to see the world.

He taught us to wear different kinds of glasses and all of a sudden we forgot about the ones we were wearing before. We just learned to stop wearing whatever kind of glasses we were looking at the world by and put on another pair.

I enjoyed this.

It was a lot of fun.

"THEM AND US"

In 1966 the "Pathways" project of the Harvard Graduate School of Education conducted a series of interviews with two groups of teenage boys. Age, family-income level, and place of residence (a public housing project in Boston) were the same for both groups of boys, but the boys in one group were white and those in the other were black. They lived on opposite sides of a street that runs through their housing project, but the groups did not know or associate with each other.

Using a tape recorder, Pathways staff member Bernard Bruce talked with both groups about their hopes for the future and their chances of realizing them. Each group then listened to the other's taped remarks and commented on them. An analysis of the boys' reactions to one another was published in the fall 1966 issue of the school's *Bulletin*.[3] This article served as a springboard for members of our field-testing group.

In preparing the material described below, John Tibbetts, Assistant Professor of Secondary Education at San Francisco State College, availed himself of the Pathways technique, not so much for purposes of diagnosis, as it was originally used, as for instruction. Tibbetts modified and developed the Harvard idea in terms of our model, concentrating on major outcomes.

The Learners

The subjects were members of two tenth-grade English classes, both consisting of "average" students. The major difference between the classes was that one came from an upper-middle-class, white, suburban community and the other drew its population from a largely Negro urban slum.

Tape interviews with members of each class revealed interesting similarities and differences. Students from both settings wanted to "get out." The suburban students found suburbia depressingly dull, despite their automobiles and social functions. "Everyone is the same," they said, and their parents, especially, were narrow and "a bore." The urban

[3] Bernard Bruce and Robert A. Rosenthal, "The World Across the Street," *Harvard Graduate School of Education Association Bulletin*, Fall 1966, pp. 3–24.

youngsters also wanted "out"—not to suburbia, but to a better section of the city, "where the action is" and where their friends were. Yet both groups acknowledged that they would probably end up living in areas very much like the ones they were in.

Concerns and Diagnosis

In the course of the episodes described below, the students provided the field-testing group with an abundance of verbal clues.

First, they indicated concern for a *positive self-image*.

URBAN STUDENTS:—I want to be the best lawyer there is, but I'll probably have to settle for some related field, like police work. I'm afraid I wouldn't make it, and I wouldn't want to put in all those years and then not make it.

—I want to be a designer, so I can mix with high society.

—I want a job where I can wear a suit and tie. Maybe I'd be willing to wear coveralls, if they be over a suit and tie.

—They [the suburban group] could buy a plain sheath dress and look dressed up, but if I bought the same dress I just wouldn't look dressed up. I don't know why it is; I just wouldn't feel dressed up without a lot of jewelry and perfume and things, you know.

—You have to dress heavily to look rich.

—We know we're overdressing; we want to prove that we *can* overdress. That's the whole point.

SUBURBAN STUDENTS:—He [a boy from the urban class] said he wanted a job where he could wear a suit. We just take it for granted that we'll go to college and get a job where you wear a suit.

—We don't want to grow up like our parents.

—When people stare at you, you think, "What's wrong with me?"

Secondly, they were concerned about *connectedness*.

URBAN STUDENTS:—They [the suburban class] said we probably weren't any different inside. But we *are* different; he's white, and I'm black, and that makes us different, both inside and out. We were raised different, and we don't feel the same things. . . . I don't mean racial prejudice, I mean we just don't talk the same jibberish.

—If we moved into their school, they'd probably look at us and our clothes for a while, and then they'd start selling their homes.

—I resent their pretending to dig our music. They say ·they like, say, the Supremes. Then if I visit them they just don't happen to have anything by the Supremes, and they start pulling out this off-the-wall music. If they don't like my music, I want them to say they don't like it. I guess some of them feel sorry for us and want us to feel accepted, and others want to feel superior, and others just don't care.

SUBURBAN STUDENTS:—If we meet those people and the topic of race comes up, what do you say? I mean how do you talk about race to, er, to someone who's colored?

—I know this colored boy, and we never talk about it. I guess he knows he's colored, but I've just never mentioned it, and I don't think I ever will.

—I know where there's a colored man living with this white lady. I don't know if they're married or not, [pause] but he keeps the lawns up nice, and they have a nice car and everything.

—We used to live in a suburb, and some Negroes moved in, and no one talked to them, and their windows got broken, and it was a kind of shame they let them move in, because no one spoke to them and their windows got broken.

Finally, they were concerned about *power.*

URBAN STUDENT:—If I went there, [to a suburban school] they'd probably say, "Get rid of him, John."
—If I don't like what he says, I'll hit him. Not because he's white, but because I don't like what he says.
—Sometimes I stop by the nursery school behind Tech and watch the kids of different races playing together, you know, and I wonder, "How much does a person have to give to make the world like that?"
SUBURBAN STUDENT: I think we're afraid to talk to them; we've heard so much about the riots and our folks telling us, "Don't go down to the X District." And they're probably afraid to talk to us, they've heard so much about the Ku Klux Klan and everything.

The cues these students gave appeared to indicate primary concerns with connectedness and its resultant power dimensions. In other words, they seemed most concerned with how individuals or groups interrelate when one is, or appears to be, very different from the other. Whether one individual or group would come out on top—would be able to say, "Get rid of him, John"—was another focus of concern.

Secondarily, there was severe alienation from parental direction and control, especially in the suburban group. One girl constantly referred to "my stupid father." Another girl, whose father refused to give her permission to meet with the urban group because he "didn't want her mixing with those niggers," managed to persuade her mother to sign the required form. Youngsters in both groups saw their parents as major deterrents to racial interaction. Negro parents were seen to act either out of fear or, at the other extreme, out of commitment to "Black Power." The white parents were seen to harbor traditional feelings of prejudice, sometimes mixed with fear and distrust. Yet some of the students appeared to harbor the very stereotypical notions for which they criticized their parents; parental influence seemed to have operated despite themselves. That this was so is evident from such cues as the suburban youngster's concern over housing problems in an integrated neighborhood and the urban youngster's concern with the suburbanites' wish to get rid of Negroes or to move away from them. Perhaps these same concerns were reflected in the urban students' insistence that, while they wanted "out" of the ghetto, they did not want to move to the suburbs.

Behavioral Outcomes

Connectedness, then, became the theme of our experiment. If students of different races and backgrounds confronted one another, would they interact in the way that their verbalization of their views would lead one to expect?

As a result of the direct confrontation, it was hoped, the students would: (1) communicate more comfortably and openly with people of different racial, religious, and socioeconomic backgrounds; (2) find common grounds for interaction with people who were in some ways different from themselves; and (3) give evidence of seeking out people different from themselves in order to explore multidimensionality.

We hoped that, when the experiences were concluded, they might make statements that would indicate the following understandings.

1) It is both possible and rewarding to discuss problems of race openly with members of different races.
2) Even where there are differences between people, there is also much that they have in common. These common factors are more important than the differences.
3) There is no reason to be afraid to interact with people from different races or socioeconomic backgrounds.

4) It is possible to demonstrate warmth and friendliness through both verbal and nonverbal behavior.

In addition, it was hoped that teachers would observe such new behavior as youngsters voluntarily mixing with members of other races and socioeconomic backgrounds, students talking openly and without embarrassment about their feelings and thoughts, and members of different races and socioeconomic levels touching one another without evidence of embarrassment or shock.

Organizers

As a result of a diagnosis based on verbal and behavioral cues, these major organizers were selected:

1) Communication between members of different races, religions, or socioeconomic backgrounds can change and expand their view of each other and themselves.
2) Some of the learned restrictions and taboos which determine responses to and thoughts about members of other groups are not accurate or valid. (Intergroup meetings, arranged for the free expression of thoughts and feelings, make it possible for members of the participating groups to test the accuracy of their ideas about each other and to revise them accordingly.)
3) Thoughts that people are most fearful of expressing often do not have the shock effect on others or the disastrous consequence anticipated.
4) People of different backgrounds, if brought together, can help each other to develop more satisfying and exciting lives by introducing their different experiences and ideas.

Content Vehicles

The content vehicles selected were (1) a film shown to each group separately on which at least one tape-recorded

discussion would be based; (2) a series of other tape recordings that could be exchanged and discussed, based on careful
questioning keyed to the organizers; and (3) a direct confrontation between the two groups on neutral ground, where
an experience equally strange to both might provide the
setting for the desired behavioral outcomes. It was hoped that
this confrontation would enable the experimenters to decide
whether verbalization is an appropriate preparation for nonverbal confrontation.

LESSON 1. The purpose of this lesson was to see if students can interact freely, physically and verbally, with other
students of different racial and socioeconomic backgrounds;
to find out how they perceive these other students, and how
this perception colors their view of themselves and their interaction with others.

The session began with a showing of the film *Prelude*,[4]
which depicts the openness and spontaneity of integrated students and programs in a unit conducted at the Philadelphia
Affective Education Project. Then the teacher told the youngsters that he would like to tape record their responses to the
film. He posed a sequence of generic questions designed to
elicit responses that would move the class from one phase of
the program to the next. (It was assumed that the regular
classroom teachers would be in the best position to translate
these questions into language most appropriate in their classrooms and to handle the responses of each class.)

The teachers' questions follow.

TEACHERS—How do you feel about what you saw and
heard in this film?
—Would you like your school to be like the
one you saw? Why?
These questions were designed to elicit the students' goals.
TEACHER:—As you think about your future, what can
you never see yourself doing?

[4] Produced by the Philadelphia Board of Education, Division of Instructional Material. This film is available as a loan at no charge except for
postage or may be purchased from the Filmmakers of Philadelphia, 1729
Sansom Street, Philadelphia, Pa.

—What *can* you see yourself doing?

—How do you feel about this?

—What plans do you have for "making it"?

Another set of questions was designed to diagnose current self-definitions.

TEACHER:—What excites you most today?

—What excites you least?

—Why do you think these things affect you like this?

—When someone you know is "turned on" by something that doesn't appeal to you, how do you feel? What do you do then?

The last group of questions were aimed at finding out how important significant adults were to the students.

TEACHER:—Are your likes and dislikes different from those of your parents and adult friends?

—Do they have plans for you that differ from your plans?

—Does it upset you to be thinking or doing things adults don't want you to do?

—If what you like to do most doesn't agree with what you're expected to do, what can you do?

—What would you do if you were confronted by a stranger whose feelings and ideas were very different from your own?

The results of this lesson are summarized under "Concerns and Diagnosis," on pages 101-4. The responses indicated that all the children wanted to get out of their existing situations, but considerable question still remained about where they might go and what they might do in the future. In general, the children rejected parental ideas and patterns but expressed the fear that they might, after all, fall into the same traps as their parents. They were quite concerned about interacting with people different from themselves; they worried about how they would look, what they would say, and, in general, what others would think of them.

LESSON 2. The same strategy and assumptions underlay this episode as the last. Questions for each class were based on the tape made by the other class during Lesson 1. The purpose was diagnostic—to help the teacher prepare for the student confrontation and determine whether the youngsters' preconceptions would be borne out when the children had a glimpse of the other group.

The teacher told the class that he had a tape recording of another group of students discussing some of the same items they had discussed earlier. He played the tape, then posed the following questions.

TEACHER:—What do you know about these students?
—How do they feel about themselves?
—What have they said that was different from what you said?
—What did they say that you have thought about a lot?
—How would you feel if you were around them much?
—Do you think they would feel the same way?
—Does it make any difference that they do or do not feel as you do?
—What do you think you would do if you met these people?
—What would you do first?

The reactions cited on pages 101-4 which refer to "they" (the other class) were taken from Lesson 2 tapes. In addition, the students made the following observations.

The suburban students thought that the students on the tape were mostly Negro and that these Negroes might be quite like them "inside." They voiced some reservations about whether they could talk to the urban children about racial problems and what would happen if they went to the same school or lived next door. They had never thought about the differences between their life goals and those of the urban children; they just took college and executive-type jobs for granted. Most of them were curious enough to want to meet the urban group.

The urban students thought that the suburban youngsters were all pretty much alike. (They also thought that they were reading their answers, because of their careful speech.) At the same time, they felt that the suburbanites were not so sophisticated (actually, "hip") as they were. They felt that it would be better for the urban group to attend the suburban high school than the other way around, because the suburban group would be more uncomfortable in the urban school than they would be in the suburban school. They were skeptical about the reaction the suburban students would have to their appearance, and they felt that they would probably have little in common to talk about. But they definitely wanted to meet.

LESSON 3. The strategy was to select neutral ground, the lawn of the local state college campus, as a confrontation site. The assumption was that such a site would be more likely to put the two groups on equal footing than a meeting at either high school. The groups were not told what to expect, but they both assumed that they would sit around and talk.

The purpose was to observe whether and how communication, verbal and nonverbal, would take place when divergent groups met on an equal footing and whether the youngsters involved would seek out more such experiences.

A warm-up session, in which the assembled students, following the instructions of a group leader, acted out reactions to a hypothetical "football game," was followed by an exercise in interaction. Each student was paired with a member of the other group. At appropriate signals from the group leader, each pair engaged in a variety of actions.

GROUP LEADER:—Look each other in the eye.
        —Partners in the first group, make a motion of any kind.
        —Partners in the second group, mirror it.
        —Try to make your partner understand something, using only your thumbs.
        —Can you say more with your elbows?

—Let's have some reactions to another football game. See if you act differently this time. (*Leader describes another game.*)

The two groups next moved to a classroom for a discussion (taperecorded) of the afternoon's events. The same group leader who had prompted the improvisations led the discussion.

GROUP LEADER:—What did you do? [*This question was necessary because the leader had not been able to observe everyone.*]

—How did you feel about interacting with strangers?

—Did you find things in common? How did this make you feel?

—Did you find differences? How did you feel about those?

—Which did you feel was more important?

—Was the group as you expected it to be?

—What conclusions can you draw from this experience?

—Will it make any difference in your feelings or in what you do when you go back?

Learning Skills

As can be seen, several principles of affective learning were successfully applied during the episodes described.

1) Emotionally charged experiences were generated through active involvement, made possible by the use of the tape recorder and the opportunities to improvise.
2) Role-playing and discussions allowed the students to imagine each other's feelings.
3) Experience was provided in a setting that offered

no threat to personal status; everyone was on equal ground, and success was virtually assured or, at the very least, failure was not probable.

4) Freedom to explore and examine the individual's role in behavioral changes was exercised in the discussions about self.

5) Change in behavior was supported by friends and respected authorities, as represented by the group leaders.

6) An opportunity was afforded to learn relevant facts. (This turned out to be the least important application of principle and was generally attended to only at the end of the sessions. Since English classes were involved, it might have been useful to direct their attention to stories and articles about successful confrontations, but time did not permit this.)

Teaching Procedures

An inductive model of recognition was applied to affective learning in an attempt to link the two areas. How the cognitive learning process was implemented in the experiment is shown below.

1) Perception (sensory)—film showing. Questions: What happened? How did you feel about it?

2) Differentiation—discussion of personal reactions to film and to tapes. Questions: Are they like you? How would you feel being around them?

3) Drawing Inferences. Questions: Why did the students on the other tape react as they did? How do you feel about that reaction?

4) Making Generalizations. Questions: What does this mean for your behavior? How would you feel if you behaved that way?

5) Application. Questions: What would you do if confrontation took place? What *did* you do when confrontation took place? How did you feel while you were doing it? Afterwards?

6) Analysis and Evaluation. Questions: What will

you do differently when you go back? Is that a good thing to do? Why?

Thus, it can be seen that the procedures used in these episodes were similar to cognitive procedures, but the content was largely affective.

Evaluation

Although the series of episodes was brief, the reactions of the students seem to indicate that it was quite successful. During the discussion which followed the confrontation, the students made such statements as

SUBURBAN STUDENT: It was good to be able to stare without feeling guilty, because we were told it was OK to do it.

URBAN STUDENT: We were like the people in the film. When we saw it, we thought it was silly, but when we *did* it, it was different. You have to do it and feel it to know something was accomplished.

SUBURBAN STUDENT: I felt my emotions were shallow. I could express disinterest or hostility without talking, but how do you express that you want to be friendly?

URBAN STUDENT: When I first saw you, I didn't like you, so I closed my hearts [sic] to you. Then when we did those things, I didn't get to know your names, but I know *you* and now I like you.

SUBURBAN STUDENT: We found that we have a lot in common, even though we didn't talk much about it.

Once, the enthusiasm of the moment was tempered by dissidence.

URBAN STUDENT: Wait a minute, you guys are getting carried away; you say that after only a little while out here twiddling thumbs and rubbing elbows you got to know the real me? That's not true. You only saw some of my inner feelings . . .

SUBURBAN STUDENT: Yes, but don't you think this could lead to better understanding?

URBAN STUDENT: Yeah, you might say we just jumped over the first fence.

There were also several observed behaviors that seemed to be significant. When the students came into the college classroom, following the outdoor improvisation, they sat around a table, completely mixed. One suburban student later remarked that if the discussion had preceded the improvisation, he was sure that all the suburban students would have sat on one side and all the urban youths on the other.

In retrospect, it seems likely that the last lesson could have been even more fruitful if there had been some preliminary role-playing in anticipation of the actual confrontation.

It might also have been helpful to exploit the fact that this was an English class by bringing in relevant literature, dialectology, structural linguistics, and so on. Unfortunately, time did not allow for this, so the hypothesis that such an effort would yield improved results cannot be stated as a certainty.

For all its shortcomings, however, the experiment generated gratifying excitement and enthusiasm. When the last session was over, the conversation in the corridors was so animated and involved that the teachers had to drag their students away. And when the students returned to their own classrooms, they begged their teachers to arrange another meeting and to let others in the school participate as well.

Nevertheless, the authors are not altogether sanguine about the possibilities for large-scale repetitions of the episodes described. For one thing, the very uniqueness of the experience might have generated a kind of "halo effect," which is not repeatable. For another, the great amount of time and money (for tape recorders, tapes, transportation) required for the experiment would, in all probability, not be available on a mass scale.

"CHAIRS": A CONCEPT OF SUBSELVES

In the course of the project, staff were fortunate to discover the work of Dr. Stewart Shapiro in ego therapy, which provided an important clue for approaching the problem of identity. Very simply, Shapiro's theory is as follows.

The self can be thought of as a cast of characters, all playing different roles, whose interaction with one another constitutes a unified self-image. The cast might include critical, loving, protecting, and observing subselves and the subself of the hurt, sorrowful child. Often these subselves war with one another, each seeking dominance over, or expulsion of, the others. As staff member Martin Haberman, now Director of Teacher Education Programs for the Central Atlantic Regional Educational Laboratory, has put it:

> These forces can be conceived of as different people who drive us to do, or not to do; to try, or not to try; to become involved, or to back off. It is as if each person is the chairman of a committee whose size varies with the situation, and one or another of whose members dominates it at any given time.

If a healthy self can be defined as one in which the subselves operate in harmonious understanding and acceptance of one another, an unhealthy self is one in which there is poor communication among the subselves, an intense desire of one or more subselves to get rid of the others, an inability to separate or distinguish one subself from another, or a superficial appreciation by subselves of others.

Using a highly imaginative and dramatic method, which he calls the "chair" technique, Shapiro has been able to help people begin to identify their own subself characters, to understand the range of forces within them, and to begin new kinds of negotiations among these forces. The following excerpt from a session in which Dr. Shapiro worked with a housewife, Mrs. B., illustrates part of his method of identifying subself characters and the roles they play.

DR. S.: What is your day like?

MRS. B.: My day . . . my days are just like every day. You know, they just . . . . Well, I clean the house and I run the children to school and back and . . .

DR. S.: Do you like those things?

MRS. B.: No, no.

DR. S.: Then why do you do them?

MRS. B.: Because I *have* to. I have a responsibility.

DR. S.: You seem to me like you are kind of trapped in this responsibility. You don't seem very enthusiastic about it.

MRS. B.: Well, I *am* trapped.

DR. S.: How do you feel about somebody that's trapped? Here, sit down (*Mrs. B. sits in one chair directly opposite an empty chair.*) Let's say that this is Diane. That's your name isn't it? . . . Diane. Tell her (*the assumed person in the empty chair*) what you think of a person—a woman like this who is trapped.

MRS. B. (*to assumed self in empty chair*): First of all, I think it's your own fault . . . and you should start accomplishing something. You never do anything. I mean, you don't even clean the house well, and you don't cook well, and you could do better, and it's *not* all your husband's fault. It's mostly your fault.

DR. S.: What do you think of her? What's your feeling?

MRS. B.: Well, I think she's lazy and I think . . . .

DR. S.: Tell her that she's lazy.

MRS. B.: I think you're lazy and I just think that you're not good for anything.

DR. S.: Can you say what you mean by that?

MRS. B.: Well, that she should get out of her rut and start doing something! And start accomplishing something and really help the children and help her husband and, uh . . . keep the house clean and not waste all of her time . . . .

DR. S.: All right, now would you sit over here (*in the empty chair*)? Now, supposing this were said to you? This (*points to original chair, now empty*) is a part of you that's saying this to you. How would you respond to that?

MRS. B.: Well, I do the best I can. It's not . . . .

DR. S.: Tell her (*pointing to empty chair*).

MRS. B.: I do the best I can. It's not my fault. It's not all of it my fault. I mean, I got married young, and no one told me that it was difficult—to be married. I thought it was just . . . you know, you get married . . . .

DR. S.: Yes?

MRS. B.: So, all this was plopped onto me all at once and . . . the adjustment started coming and everything got confused and I . . . . Everything wasn't all my fault. It wasn't all my fault. I'm doing the best I can.

DR. S.: You're doing the best you can.

MRS. B.: Yes.

DR. S.: All right, now would you sit over here please (*in a third chair*)? Now, supposing you were an outside observer and you saw these two people talking, what would you see? What can you observe between this person and this person?

MRS. B.: Well, this person . . . .

DR. S.: Which one?

MRS. B.: This one (*points to original empty chair*) keeps making excuses and doesn't take any of the criticism, and yet this person (*indicates other empty chair*) is criticizing and it's not . . . it's nothing constructive. They're not really communicating.

DR. S.: Now, who is making the excuses for this one (*points to original empty chair*)? She's making her own excuses?

MRS. B.: Uhuh, yes.

DR. S.: Is she sort of defending herself against this criticism?

MRS. B.: Nothing's happening there.

DR. S.: Is she feeling sorry for herself, by the way?

MRS. B.: Yes.

DR. S.: All right, now you be the person right there (*points to another chair*) that feels sorry for this poor girl that's a housewife and has to do all these things. Tell her (*original chair*) how you feel about her.

MRS. B.: Well, you do the best you can, and you try to look nice, and you cook with the money you have, and you can't buy steak, and so you make stew and you . . . .

DR. S.: What are you saying to her?

MRS. B.: You're doing the best you can.

DR. S.: You're not so bad, huh?

MRS. B.: No-o.

DR. S.: I appreciate you. Is that what you're saying?

MRS. B.: Yes.

DR. S.: Tell her.

MRS. B.: I appreciate you. I think you're doing just fine the way you are.

DR. S.: OK. Now, would you sit over in this chair [a fourth] please? Now again, as the observer, what do you see here?

MRS. B.: I can see three different personalities.

DR. S.: What are these three different kinds of personalities?

MRS. B.: Well, I guess this one (*pointing to the original chair*) is the one that's actually moving—actually doing things and making excuses for herself. This one (*pointing to second chair*) is criticizing, and this one (*pointing to third chair*) is loving . . . .

DR. S.: Sort of taking her [*original chair*] part?

MRS. B.: Protecting . . . . Yes, uhuh.

DR. S.: Protecting . . . very good. Thank you very much.[5]

Although Dr. Shapiro's method was designed as therapy for disturbed adults, it can be profitably used with people having no serious emotional difficulties. Reading about this and witnessing similar situations led us to consider the possibility of adapting the technique to ordinary classroom situations.

The concept of subselves struck us immediately as a valuable organizing idea. It seemed ideal for the many children whose concept of self is so undifferentiated that when something goes wrong, such as failing a math test, total self-condemnation results. "I failed math, therefore I'm stupid, therefore I'm a worthless person" becomes their refrain, rather than, "I failed math, therefore I may not be so good in math, but I'm still worthwhile because there are other parts of me that do all right in other things."

An implied teaching objective would be to help the child realize his differentiated self by first having him become aware that there are such things as subselves.

The following report, by Professor Haberman and Judith Davies, an English teacher at a Racine, Wisconsin, high

[5] Stewart B. Shapiro, "Transactional Aspects of Ego Therapy," *Journal of Psychology*, LVI (1963), 487–89.

school, is an attempt to introduce the notion of differentiated subselves through literature. This particular episode, specifically designed to teach literature, seems to offer an excellent approach to that subject and helps students to get inside a character. It stops short, however, of making the connection between the subselves of the literary characters and the students' own committee of subselves. In that respect, it fails the model's objective to deal with the students' concerns for self-identity.

Despite this failure and the absence of raw data in the form of student-teacher dialogue, the episode is included here because it can be a valuable first step in helping to establish a satisfying self-concept.

Let's Play "Chairs"

Many high-school graduates claim the dubious distinction of having completed their schooling without ever reading a book. For some, it might be correct to add, "or thought any idea through."

But this is a mixed crew. Some of these graduates are not able students; some are from impoverished backgrounds; many have high potential but have not developed the skills of "schoolmanship" to the point of making good grades. Many others, however, are from the ranks of the "silent advanced." These are highly capable youngsters who have become alienated or, at least, disengaged from school programs, teachers, and in some cases the world at large. They do the minimum needed to graduate, but not much more.

To get these youngsters to read, think, and talk more, we used a game called "Chairs," suggested by Dr. Shapiro's work. As teachers, it seemed to us that this game could be used to help high-school seniors understand more about characters in books and to make them want to read more. It would be natural, we thought, for students to use new insights gained from playing "Chairs" not only to understand what drives fictional characters to act as they do but also to explain and predict their own behavior. Nevertheless, we avoided using the game for counseling or guidance. Our objective was to improve the teaching of literature by sensitizing students to the conflicts within well-developed literary characters. We believed that genuine appreciation, like real education, would have a personally significant meaning for the individual student, but that it was up to him to determine these meanings for himself and in his own way. We concentrated on characters in books and trusted that the student would privately personalize whatever part of the character analysis touched him.

Unlike role-playing, in which several students play different characters, "Chairs" is played by one person—preferably a volunteer—taking all the subparts within a single individual. He begins by sitting in a chair and talking like the character in a story. When he reaches some discrepancy or conflict in the character, he sets up another chair and has a dialogue with it. This discussion among an individual's subparts can become a trio, a quartet, and so on, and can even include contributions from other chairs representing forces outside the character which impinge on his behavior.

Initially, the teacher assumes responsibility for asking the questions of the volunteer playing "Chairs." Members of the class also ask questions and suggest points where the player might introduce a new chair (that is, the points where a student seems to be introducing into his monologue one of the literary character's different subselves).

The basic process consists of establishing a character and his conflict by eliciting comments from the volunteer that will delineate areas of uncertainty in the character. Usually, about ten minutes of casual give-and-take is required for the conflicting attitudes to become apparent. Then the player alternates between expressing the conflicting attitudes, telling his other chairs when they are wrong and why, and commenting on how it feels to be espousing whatever his role of the moment might be. The chairs are encouraged to press their conflicts with one another until the various attitudes are obvious and the strengths of each are clear.

At times, no attitude is clearly dominant in a given chair, and special techniques must be used to determine its relative strength. For example, conflicting chairs can be asked to convince a yet undecided chair to choose a viewpoint. The player may be asked to stand up and view the various possibilities, and then take the chair he feels most comfortable with, the one whose sentiments he could most freely express. Or a student can indicate the strength of various chairs literally by force—by pushing the hands of the questioner to indicate the degree to which he holds the view expressed.

Observations

During the course of many "Chairs" games, several clues to more successful "games" became evident.

1) Students are often hazy about the details of the novels being analyzed. In order to discourage them from simply projecting whatever they wish into the characters, a brief introductory discussion should be held in which all the students participate in establishing the characters.

2) Students cannot really keep a successful "Chairs" conversation going if they think of it in the past tense. Choosing a character from a book that is still being read by the class is preferable to taking one from a book that has already been read.

3) Inner conflicts which have not been resolved by the author's "right" answer, such as Lady Macbeth's, offer the best kind of subject matter.

4) Players may run out of ideas and thus be unable to get very far with a character. Substituting another character from the same book will sometimes refurbish their arsenals of ideas.

5) Books that are not very well written, in which motives are muddy or problems are not real, are difficult for students to work with. As this becomes clear, the technique proves valuable for judging literary quality.

6) An opportunity to discuss both the book and the "Chairs" process seems to be needed after the player has exhausted all arguments. The discussion may

deal with misinterpretations of the character, with reactions to the arguments advanced or their outcomes, or with the entire book.

Evaluation

Students read more. They become more sensitive to the conflict of motives in authors' characterizations. They begin to look for "Chairs" situations as they read, and their understanding of the multiple facets of a personality becomes much clearer after participating in the game. Within three months of the introduction of "Chairs," for example, a group of eleven "silent advanced" students had read a total of sixty-nine books. Several students said that they had never really understood what they read until they had observed, or played out, a character for themselves.

5

THREE
DIAGNOSTIC
TECHNIQUES

In early discussions of the model, members of the field-testing group and other discussants sought diagnostic techniques for the classroom that would help them to elicit and analyze cues to the three concerns we have been examining: identity, power, and connectedness. Toward this end, we devised three new techniques: "Faraway Island," "Ten Years from Now," and "Time Capsule." Initially, we supposed that they would be purely diagnostic. As we worked with them, however, it developed that they were not equally effective in diagnosing concerns, but that all of them could be most useful as rudimentary instructional devices or content vehicles. Nevertheless, in many respects, the techniques retain their diagnostic quality. Several teachers have found that they furnish information that helps them to base teaching decisions on learners' concerns. On occasion, teachers have been able to use the children's responses about how they cope with their concerns to select teaching content in terms of these concerns.

In the sense that they get children to talk about themselves, the people they live with, and the aspects of their lives which they feel are most significant, these are learning techniques for both students and teachers. The temptation to put them to other uses is apparent, but we would rather see them used as stagings for teaching decisions and for the building of more elaborate structures based on concerns than for "psyching out" the students.

THE "FARAWAY ISLAND"

The "Faraway Island" technique was developed by Gerald Weinstein and used to help children become more aware of, and articulate, the criteria they use for attaching significance to other people. Assuming that everybody has a concern for connectedness, we wanted to learn what factors make some people more significant than others to the students involved. What people would they choose to be connected with—to spend their lives with—and why? A well-known television interviewer recently remarked that she has several provocative questions she usually asks celebrities, one of which is: "If you were recuperating in a hospital, who would you want to be in the bed next to you, excluding relatives?" [1] This question, like the Faraway Island technique, is designed to uncover what the respondent values or looks for in others, and can bring to consciousness significant assumptions about how and why he chooses his friends.

The following instructions were used to introduce this exercise to two different groups of children.

Assume that you have to spend the rest of your life on

[1] Barbara Walters of the NBC *Today* show, as reported in *The New York Times*, July 2, 1967, p. 15.

a remote island with just six people and no one else. Imagine that! None of these six people can be anyone you already know, but you're allowed to specify what they should be like. What kinds of people would you pick to live the rest of your life with? You might think about how old they'd be, their sex, the things they'd like to do and the things they wouldn't like to do, their personalities, their looks, or any other qualities. Assume, also, that all your basic needs are taken care of, so you don't have to scrounge around for food, clothing, and shelter. All you have to do is describe as fully as you can what the people you'd choose to live with would be like.

Following are transcripts of the dialogues that took place with two groups of children, the first a racially mixed group, aged 15 and 16, enrolled in an Upward Bound project in Hoboken, New Jersey.

FIRST GIRL: First I'd pick a doctor in case I get sick. It could be anybody, as long as they're nice and can be trusted. Just as long as I have the doctor first.
LEADER: You wouldn't care if they were all men?
FIRST GIRL: No. I would pick men and women.
LEADER: All the same age?
FIRST GIRL: They'd have to be young. I wouldn't want them to be old. They'd pass away any time. I want everybody to live as long as I do.

LEADER: Any other ideas, anybody?
FIRST BOY: I would like to live with six other people, like Victor, say. They're willing and able to sit down and talk, discuss at any time, like Victor. We're very close friends and all. He's willing to sit down and tell me his problems and I tell him mine. Like that. We'll do anything, I'm quite sure we will. That's how close we are. Now these six people I'd pick wouldn't care if there were no women, because, you know, I'm not planning to get married.
LEADER: So, these would be six men. And tell me about the other people in the group.

FIRST BOY: Well, they'd all have to be working because they'd all have to come up with an equal amount of rent, you know. So I would pick people that know what they're talking about and not no dumb person . . . you know, you're talking about certain subjects and they're wandering. I would get six people same as Victor, his personality and everything, his actions and like that.

LEADER: Anybody else?

FIRST BOY: I would like one or two people that's older than I. Can't be anybody I know. I would like a person like a college professor that's hip. He knows what's happening and all, and you know he's smart, and he could keep order in case anything happens, you know. Let's say two older people, two girls, in the same age bracket, understanding, and what not. And then another guy around my age. And I would like these to possess qualities and be able to do things. Maybe one is musically inclined and has talent and you could do this. And another one draws, you know, things that would keep you busy.

SECOND BOY: I would like to have one older guy that's real smart. . . . He'd pick a part and argue like mad. You couldn't put nothing over on him. And I'd like a guy and a girl around my age that I could talk with that would be good conversations.

LEADER: What's a good conversation?

SECOND BOY: Like being interested in what I'm interested in. Like they'd have to be smart, like we all know one another, we all know what we're interested in, like music. We can talk about politics and everybody can understand each other.

LEADER: Would you make any different choices than they did?

SECOND GIRL: Yeah, a little girl and a little boy. You know, you could watch them grow up and everything. Teach them how to walk and talk and everything.

LEADER: So the two kids would be part of your group?

SECOND GIRL: Yes. Then two men and two women my

age. You know, like Bob Hope. Someone who'd make you laugh, like a comedian, instead of just having conversation, boring me. Somebody like that, somebody that would make you laugh.

LEADER: How much different or the same would the people be in terms of you? Would you try to pick people who were as much like you as possible, or who were very different?

SECOND GIRL: The same, I guess, my same age and things like that. I don't mean everybody has to be Spanish or everybody has to be colored.

THIRD GIRL: I don't think everybody could be the same as you, because it's a known fact that people cannot live with themselves. They have to find somebody different to get along with them. You can't have too much in common with a person. They might have something in common with you, but they'll have a different idea and you'll end up in an argument.

LEADER: What would the people that were different do?

THIRD GIRL: Well, they'll try to show us something that they know about, and, at the same time, we could be showing them something that we know about.

SECOND GIRL: Well, as far as nationality is concerned, I could live with any nationality just as long as they're not segregated, you know what I mean?

LEADER: How would your group of six be segregated? What would be a segregated group?

SECOND GIRL: You know, like, they don't like all nationalities but one, and yours is a different nationality.

LEADER: But what would you select? You're the one who has to make the selection.

SECOND GIRL: Well, I would select the Spanish, like she says, Negroes. I guess I'd select a white as long as it would have nothing against the Spanish or Negroes.

THIRD BOY: Are you going to be able to go on the outside world?

LEADER: Not too much; they're really stuck.

THIRD BOY: But do they know what's happening on the

outside world? Because like now, she took people who aren't segregated, and you kept on finding out what's happening, like with civil rights, like bombing the houses in Alabama, like they killed this guy, and they kill that guy, and Martin Luther King says this and says that. That might all change the people. I think that no matter who you pick, something might happen if you get news from the outside world.

SECOND GIRL: I don't think they will because they'd know they would have to live with us. It's like you said, all their life, and I don't think they'll change like that because they know if they change they'll get to fighting and arguing, and they aren't going to want to hear it all the time.

THIRD BOY: They're only human.

The second group consisted of white 12- and 13-year-olds who were enrolled in a private school in New York City.

FIRST BOY: I would like them to have something in common with me so we'd have something to talk about but also to have some variances so we can get to see all points of view. And people who aren't too far out, like those who take LSD or real beatniks, but not really . . . more free than the types of people who spend their lives and all the time they do this and do that.

LEADER: You mean not too conventional and not too far out?

FIRST BOY: Right.

LEADER: Can you give me an idea of their ages, their sex?

FIRST BOY: I'd like their age to be fairly near mine, and sex—three boys and three girls.

LEADER: All the same age?

FIRST BOY: Yes, within two years.

FIRST GIRL: They wouldn't all be the same age. They could be any age. And pretty well divided as to sex, I guess. They couldn't be bigoted. They'd have to have sort of romantic notions about life, like love and peace and all that stuff, but not too much so I could sort of convince them. I like to convince people. And they'd have to be sort of way out so they wouldn't be restricted by convention and they could do what they want.

LEADER: You said any age. So in other words you could have six three-year-olds?

FIRST GIRL: Well, I didn't mean three-year-olds. I mean from about 14 or 15 and up.

LEADER: How old would be the limit on top?

FIRST GIRL: I don't know. Dead.

LEADER: So it might be a 90-year-old swinger? OK, are there any other qualities you can imagine? Physical characteristics? How different or the same from you?

FIRST GIRL: I don't care what they look like. As long as they're not too sick in the head and don't get on other people's nerves. I couldn't stand that.

FIRST BOY: I think I'd like to have them in age from around 12 to 16, not too old or they might die, and then I wouldn't have anyone to be with any more, and if you're alone for the rest of your life, you would go crazy. And I think they'd have to have some appreciation for nature; but I wouldn't like it if they were the kind of people who thought man should keep building all over the place and making jets and things like that.

LEADER: You'd want them to all feel that way?

FIRST BOY: Well, not all, but I wouldn't want them to feel completely like that, but I wouldn't want any of them to be exaggerated one way or the other. Sex—half boys and half girls. Ages—12 to 16, around there.

LEADER: How about you?

SECOND GIRL: I would like them to be the conventional type. I wouldn't want them to be too far out. And I would like them to be able to talk about a lot of interesting things. Each one of us might have something different to talk to the others about. And we would all get along. Divided equally three and three.

LEADER: How would these people feel? Would they have any qualities or feelings you might ask for?

SECOND GIRL: Not to be phony.

LEADER: What do you mean by "phony"?

SECOND GIRL: Not putting on airs and not being themselves. They must have a sense of humor.

LEADER: Would they have any particular skills?

SECOND BOY: I'd like them to be about my age. To be, three of them, to be people that I work with in music and equally divided, and I'd like them to look up to me.

LEADER: You'd want them to have respect and think you're pretty good. Any other qualities you can think of, any other ideas?

SECOND BOY: I'd like them to have an even temperament so that they're not always fighting each other. And they should all have their own individual main interest, like I like history, and maybe another one will like math. We should share some common interests. They should all like nature and the outdoors.

LEADER: No insiders, eh?

SECOND GIRL: They all have to love each other, but not in the way that they all get silly ties and everything, so that if one of them wants to go away and marry someone, they wouldn't all get upset.

SECOND BOY: I think that the people should of course like each other but they shouldn't be people who get involved to such an extent that they get hurt.

Evaluation

Looking at the responses from the New York City and Hoboken groups, we see two distinct patterns. The Upward Bound students chose people who could exercise control over situations and events—a doctor "in case I get sick," a college professor that's hip, he knows what's happening and all . . . he's smart, and he could keep order in case anything happens," and only people who were working because they would "all have to come up with an equal amount of rent." People who have the greatest control over life were considered to be the most significant.

Such people were not central to the private school students. The difference may stem from the difference in economic security between the two groups. The data are true to Maslow's hierarchy of needs, according to which security and safety needs are prior to love and belonging needs.[2] In any case, the experiences of the Hoboken group seem to have imposed a Hobbesian world view, in which everyone, including oneself, is seen as needing strong external controls. This group seemed to feel that the island society could easily revert to a state of nature, and its members wanted people around who would ensure control and regularity. The children in the private-school group expressed less need for control and perhaps less awareness of the survival needs; they seemed to trust themselves and those like them to keep life safe and under control.

The private-school group wanted to exclude people who were "too far out." Although these students didn't want the company of conventional, conforming people, they did want to keep extremists out. They wanted people to "be themselves. . . be free . . . not be phony . . . not be too far out"; a far-out person's actions are unpredictable and he cannot be relied on or trusted. Perhaps the students equated "far-out-ness" with deviance and were seeking creative, unconventional people who were nevertheless not deviant. In any case, for these youngsters, the island society would be peaceful and harmonious only if the people there were like themselves—not too conformist and not too unconventional.

The Upward Bound group was less concerned about unconventionality and deviance. Members of this group seemed more sensitive to the value of differences, as was the girl who remarked: "It's a known fact that people cannot live with themselves. They have to find somebody different to get along with them." This difference was important to her because it meant "They'll try to show us something that they know about, and, at the same time, we could be showing them something we know about." The Hoboken boy who noted that knowledge of the outside world can change people, "no

[2] Abraham H. Maslow, "A Theory of Human Development," *Psychological Review*, L (1943), 370–96.

matter who you pick," obviously sensed that difference, deviance, and disorder are in many ways situationally created.

The private-school group wanted a frictionless society. For them, peace is equivalent to lack of critical differences and to being involved only when it doesn't hurt. One girl, for example, said that the islanders would "all have to love each other, but not in the way that they all get silly ties and everything, so that if one of them wants to go away and marry someone, they wouldn't all get upset." One of the boys said that people should like each other "but they shouldn't be people who get involved to such an extent they get hurt."

If peace can exist only when there is no conflict, or if people should be involved only when there's no chance of being hurt, then peace and involvement become unattainable. The early development of such an outlook may lead to unfounded cynicism and apathy, the feeling that action will not make a difference. People with this outlook often spend their lives desperately waiting for a time when there will be no conflict, pain, or sorrow. A goal for teachers of such children might be to search with them for strategies for attaining peace in conflict situations and finding new ways of relating to people.

Except for one girl who would lock out bigoted islanders, the private-school group offered no specifications for the racial composition of their island. The Hoboken students, on the other hand, talked quite a bit about segregation and race; for them it was an immediate, pressing issue. For the private-school students, whose daily lives were not immediately affected by race, it was not.

Students in both groups wished to exclude old people because they did not want death to deprive them of companionship; most of them wanted all the islanders to be about their own age or a little older. The desire of the Hoboken girl for a "little girl and a little boy," so that she "could watch them grow up . . . teach them how to walk and talk and everything," paralleled the desire of the New York girl for islanders with "romantic notions about life . . . but not too much so I could sort of convince them." Adding, "I like to convince people," this girl, like the other, wanted to teach and perhaps reach others. Both girls seemed to feel that they had skills and knowledge that were valuable and worth passing on. Students in both groups wanted bright, articulate people on their island, valuing those who could reason and argue. Awareness of events and the ability to talk about them were prized qualities.

Both groups were somewhat limited in their appreciation of the differences among people. They saw only that some people are intelligent and others are not; that some are far out, some conventional, and others in between; that some have control over events and others are powerless. There was a tendency to see most differences in extreme categories of good and bad.

Suggested Teaching Procedures

The teacher must ask himself how he can best help his students to recognize and value a variety of differences between people. He might begin by having his students make their own survey of the ways in which people are different. He might ask

—How can two 21-year-old men, both of whom are intelligent and not too far out and both of whom have some control over events, be different from each other?

—How might identical twins be different from each other?

—Could you possibly want to have one on your island and not the other?

Phyllis and Terry,[3] a film about two teenage girls living on the Lower East Side of New York City, might be used to initiate such a discussion, providing a common reference point.

Once students have a wider understanding of the ways in which people are different, the teacher can help them to investigate the significance of these differences. Asking the students which girl, Phyllis or Terry, they would prefer for

[3] Distributed by the Center for Mass Communication of Columbia University Press, a 16 mm film, black and white.

their island sets the stage for further discussion. Whichever one they choose, the students should be encouraged to articulate the reasons for their preference in order to develop a clearer concept of their own patterns of choice.

Next, the teacher might help the students to examine their choices for clues about themselves. Gardner Murphy's "How We Come to Want What We Want" [4] is good background reading for the teacher. Eventually the students should examine the differences between the people they choose for the island and the people with whom they spend their time. They can be helped with such questions as

—Are the island people very different from your friends? If so, what might that tell you about yourself?

—What have you learned about yourself if both the island group and the here-and-now group are alike?

—Do you in either case want to change the people you spend your time with and what you do with it?

Reading Herbert A. Otto's "Friendship Action Method," [5] a technique of analyzing one's choices (and rejections) of friends, can further help students to analyze their current friendship structures and the criteria they use.

"TEN YEARS FROM NOW"

In another approach to the discovery of concerns, students were asked what they thought they would be doing and what they would be like "ten years from now." Having made their predictions, the students were asked to answer two key questions: "How will you get there?" (or "What steps should you take to get there?") and "What are your *real* chances of getting there?" Discrepancies between the ideal (what the student would like to be) and the real (what he thought he would be) were often made salient

[4] In *Human Potentialities,* (New York: Basic Books, 1958), Chap. 5.
[5] In *Group Methods Designed to Actualize Human Potential* (Salt Lake City: University of Utah, 1967), pp. 79–81.

through this technique. In general, while the student's sense of identity and connectedness tended to surface with this approach, what became most apparent was the degree of power or control he thought he had over his own destiny.

This technique was used with the previously described groups of Upward Bound and private-school students. Transcripts of the tape-recorded sessions between Mr. Weinstein and each of the groups follow.

Upward Bound

LEADER: Think of yourself ten years from now. Try to picture that. What I'd like you to do is try to describe the picture you have of yourself ten years from now, in any way you can. How would you like to see yourself in ten years?

FIRST BOY: A writer, a reporter, I wouldn't get married, I'd travel.

LEADER: So, you'd be a bachelor, a writer, and you'd be traveling around?

FIRST BOY: Yes, I'd write about the people I see, the people I knew. The trouble is right now I don't have anything to write about.

LEADER: Is there anything else you can do to clear up the picture? So far I know you're a bachelor and you're traveling around, writing.

FIRST BOY: That's about the general idea.

LEADER: Where would you be living?

FIRST BOY: I'd just be traveling around.

LEADER: What kind of people would you be associating with?

FIRST BOY: Any kind, I like to meet all types.

FIRST GIRL: I want to be a surgical nurse.

LEADER: A surgical nurse. Tell me about what else you might look like or be like ten years from now.

FIRST GIRL: I'll be real skinny and real old. I'll be twenty-six.

LEADER: Are you going to be married?

FIRST GIRL: No.

LEADER: Why not?

FIRST GIRL: I don't want to get married. I'll get married when I'm about thirty-five.

FIRST BOY: Nobody will want an old woman, an old bag.

FIRST GIRL: If you get married when you're nineteen, you'll get tied down and have kids and everything.

SECOND GIRL: I want to be a gym teacher. I don't know why. Like she said, I don't want to get married.

LEADER: Ever?

SECOND GIRL: Yeah, but not right now. I want to have fun.

LEADER: You do want to get married, but not necessarily ten years from now. What do you see yourself doing besides teaching gym?

SECOND GIRL: I guess going out a lot, not like going out at night, like traveling to schools and teaching.

THIRD GIRL: Sometimes I see myself as a secretary, going to France or something. Then sometimes I see myself as a teacher, teaching either an English class or a steno class, and I'm not married. Sometimes I see myself engaged.

LEADER: What's the fear about marriage here? You're engaged but not married.

THIRD GIRL: Because engagements can be broken. But not marriage. Engagements give you a chance to know about the person. Marriage means you're tied down to one person, and you have to know enough about him to make sure you're willing to make sacrifices.

LEADER: And don't you think the possibility is good that you *can* know enough about him?

THIRD GIRL: Well, after a while. You can't just tell how someone is when you just meet them. You have to get to know them.

SECOND BOY: In ten years, I would like to see myself as a chief executive of a profit-making organization or either as a nuclear physicist, because I'm very interested in all types of sciences or that field, because ever since sixth grade, when I started to know what science was, I've become interested in it a lot.

LEADER: Well, what about your personal self, that's your professional self.

SECOND BOY: I'm going to be a bachelor. I don't want no women to be holding me down. This is the changing world of progress, you know. Women would be holding you down. Don't go here, and don't go there. I don't want to hear that.

LEADER: You don't have as much freedom?

SECOND BOY: That's right. They hold you down from a lot of things.

THIRD BOY: I don't know what I'll do. It all depends on whether I get in college or not. If I get in college, I want to get a real good job and make as much money as I can. I don't want to be a millionaire, but I want to make enough money to live comfortably.

LEADER: You don't care what you have to do to make it?

THIRD BOY: I won't be bloodthirsty or anything, but I want what I guess all people call a good job.

LEADER: Anything else about yourself, besides your job, that you'd like to see in ten years?

THIRD BOY: I guess I'll be maried. I don't mind getting married. I may have a couple of kids by then.

LEADER: What kind of a house do you see yourself living in?

THIRD BOY: Kind of suburban. I don't know. I like the city and all, but it's not too good for the kids, although I grew up in the city, and I didn't come out that bad.

LEADER: Anything else you see?

THIRD BOY: I don't know. Not much more. I'll have a nice car and all.

LEADER: OK, you kids have told me something you'd like to see happen. You said you want to be a writer and travel around. What do you have to do to get there? You told me what you want to be. What do you have to do to get there?

FIRST BOY: Probably take courses in high school that give you a chance to write, journalism, creative writing. Enter contests that they hold. Write for magazines like maybe *Junior Scholastic*. If you write a story, you might get it in there or in other magazines. You might be getting paid for that, and it would be a start. When you go to college, maybe you could major in English, be in discussion groups, you know. A lot of that kind of thing.

LEADER: Do you have a pretty good idea of how you would get to be a surgical nurse, what you'd have to do?

FIRST GIRL: After I graduate from high school I'd go to nursing school for four years and study. And every day I'd be at the hospital and learn the routine.

SECOND GIRL: I know I'd have to get a college education for four years. I might as well do it, because your friends are still in school and you might as well go to college. If you get out of high school and don't go to college you'd just be around the streets. It's better for you to go to college.

LEADER: Most all of you said that what you want to do would require some college in order to get a good job. What chances do you think you really have of going to college?

SECOND GIRL: Not very big. Unless the government will allow you to take out enough money to put you through college. They won't give you all the money.

FIRST BOY: I thought you meant scholastically, not financially.

LEADER: No, anything, whatever it takes to get through college. Do you think you're going to get through, to make it all the way up that line?

SECOND GIRL: I always wanted to be a teacher, but with my marks, I don't even know if I'll get through high school.

SECOND BOY: I think I'd have a good chance because I've had these two years of biology and chemistry. My teachers both have said that I have a very good chance of going to college, so I think I have a very good chance.

LEADER: Do you think you could swing it financially, too?

SECOND BOY: Oh, yes, I think I could, because my parents would pay for my college fees and what not.

LEADER: Talk to me about the rest of your real chances of making it ten years from now.

SECOND GIRL: Well, I want to go to college, but I don't want my mother to pay for it. I want to pay for it myself. I guess when I get out of school I'll have to get a job and whatever I make, I'll save it all, won't spend nothing of it until I get the amount I need.

LEADER: And you think you'll be able to do that?

SECOND GIRL: No, because I know that when I get it and see something I want, I'm going to spend it.

SIXTH BOY: My chances are pretty bad scholastically. I got a good IQ and all, but my school marks are very bad. I was doing OK, like passing but not real great. But not this year. It is very bad. It's shot.

LEADER: What do you think your chances are?

SIXTH BOY: Well, first financially, I want my father to help and my mother to help. My father says he'll help me through college. He wants me to go to college to make the best out of it. And why I want him to help me is because he underestimates me. Like he sees my report card, he sees two seventies or three seventies on it. I'm not failing. But he'd say "Oh, look at this. If you keep this up in high school, how are you going to get to college?" I think that I could make it scholastically. I think my marks are all right.

LEADER: Do you think even if they wanted to help you financially they could support you through college? Do you know how much college costs?

SIXTH BOY: It varies. You could go to a junior college, maybe.

LEADER: What do you do about that? You all have a ten-year dream, and then when I ask you what your chances are of making it, it doesn't sound very positive. How do you live with that?

FIRST GIRL: Try to change. Try to better youself.

LEADER: How?

THIRD GIRL: Make sure you know what you're doing.

LEADER: How do you do that?

THIRD GIRL: Let's say going to secretary school. Going to that, I have to have steno and typing, definitely, unless I take bookkeeping or some other things. Make sure I know what I'm talking about, what I'm doing, so that after I graduate, I'll be able to get a part-time job or full-time job as a secretary, and sometimes those jobs send you to secretarial school.

LEADER: So, you think that's a way out for you, when you say you have to know what you're doing while you're still in high school and get those skills, stenographic skills and so forth? Do you know what you're doing now?

THIRD GIRL: Most of the time.

LEADER: So you really don't have to change anything.

THIRD GIRL: Partly, yeah.

LEADER: What do you do with that, the dream and the chances?

SECOND GIRL: Once you get out of school, you can try. Trying never hurts. I'm not saying you're going to make it. But at least try. By working, you might just make it. You might be able to pay for the whole thing.

LEADER: You know you had your dream and then you told me what your chances were. They didn't sound too good.

FIRST GIRL: Chances of going to college or being a nurse? You don't have to go to college to be a nurse.

LEADER: Surgical nurse, I thought you said.

FIRST GIRL: You have to go to a nursing school.

SECOND GIRL: That's just as bad as college.

FIRST GIRL: But it isn't all that hard.

LEADER: How do you know?

FIRST GIRL: Because my girlfriend's sister is a nurse. She lives in California, and she had to take the exam, right? She took it, and she failed, and they let her take it again. So it can't be all that hard, if they let her take it again. The college boards you can't take over.

LEADER: Does she have to pay to go to nursing school?

FIRST GIRL: No. I don't know. Sometimes they send you. If you're real good they send you.

LEADER: They send you? Are you real good?

FIRST GIRL: No. So, I'll have to pay.

LEADER: What do you really think will happen with you?

FIRST GIRL: I'll be a nurse. My father will send me to nursing school. He wanted me to go to college, and I said, "No," because of my marks.

LEADER: And with those marks you can go to nursing school?

FIRST GIRL: No, but to be a nurse all you have to do is have chemistry, biology, algebra, and I'm passing them. You know what I got on my biology? A 95.

Private School

LEADER: I imagine everyone has a picture of what they might be doing, of what they might want to be like in the future. So, I'm going to ask you to picture yourself ten years from now. I am sure some of you have the picture already of what you might like to be like or doing at that time. I wonder if you could begin telling me what that picture is like. Yourself—ten years from now.

FIRST BOY: I've changed a lot of times, of course, and now I'm kind of interested in birds, so when I look at the colleges and things like that, I think I'd like to go to Cornell University, which has a program in ornithology there. And then they also have a laboratory where I could continue in that work.

LEADER: Can you tell me a little bit about the picture? You'll be going to Cornell and studying ornithology. What else do you see about yourself at that time?

FIRST BOY: I think before getting married I'd like to just live for a while and look around me and things like that before I decide what I want. I'd decide what I want first and then . . . .

LEADER: You do intend to get married?

FIRST BOY: Yes.

LEADER: Do you think that if you got married before you had a chance to look around, you wouldn't be able to look around?

FIRST BOY: I'd rather look around before I commit myself.

LEADER: Can you tell me anything else about where you might be living or what you might be like as a person?

FIRST BOY: I can't really think what I might be like as a person. I think I'd still like to live in New York City, possibly in the Village.

SECOND BOY: Well, I'm interested in history, so I'd like to go to college and study history and go for a teacher's degree after that. And before I settle down I'd probably like to go to Europe or different places around the world first. Then come back and either live in New York or move out to the West Coast. I really can't say what I'd be like ten years from now. I can't tell now.

LEADER: Do you think you'll be married?

SECOND BOY: Well, I don't know. I guess I'd like to be married, but not too early. I'd like to wait for a while, live by myself for a while.

THIRD BOY: Well, I'm interested in music, and I kind of picture myself ten years from now traveling around the country and playing in an orchestra and meeting new people. I was sort of considering the Peace Corps for a while, and I think I'd like to go into the army, probably after high school or after college.

LEADER: Why the army?

THIRD BOY: Either the army or the navy, into the service.

LEADER: You mean instead of the Peace Corps?

THIRD BOY: No, I'd like to develop, but I have to serve, so I'd like to get it over with before I go into a career.

LEADER: Anything else about who you might be with ten years from now?

THIRD BOY: I don't want to get married until I really have been around.

FIRST GIRL: I've got lots of things. I may be a teacher or join VISTA, and I don't know whether I'll be out of school at that time. Maybe I'll take a master's degree. I want to hitchhike across the country.

LEADER: You want to hitchhike across the country. Why?

FIRST GIRL: I don't know.

LEADER: Do you see yourself settling down at any time with a family or anything?

FIRST GIRL: I don't know when.

LEADER: Do you see yourself as any different from what you are now, as a person?

FIRST GIRL: More experience.

LEADER: More experience. What would that be?

FIRST GIRL: I don't know. I really can't tell.

SECOND GIRL: I'm really not too sure. I'm interested in fashion designing, so I might go where they have a good art program for fashion. I'd like to live with a roommate for a while, and try for a career and see how it is and then settle down.

LEADER: Did any of you mention anything that didn't require college?

THIRD BOY: I said I wanted to be in the service, and then I want to go to college.

LEADER: To study what?

THIRD BOY: Music and regular college courses, too.

LEADER: How clearly can you tell me the steps required to get where you want to be ten years from now? Do you know what you have to do?

FIRST BOY: Well, going to college you have to keep up your marks while you're in high school and your average and things like that. And then, on the entrance exams, do well enough to get in college. And then from there you have to try to learn as much about the field you want to go in and do your own experimenting.

LEADER: Is this going to cost you money?

FIRST BOY: Yes, going to college, of course, unless you're going to a city college. Some don't cost anything.

FOURTH BOY: My sister's going to college next year, and I can imagine what it's going to be like for me, because she's been looking through catalogues and trying to find a college she would like to go to. She's been taking tests, and she finally decided on one in Ohio. They accepted her, and she had to go out and visit it before she was accepted and make a good impression. I think it's been pretty hard on her. Now this summer, she's going to have to work to save up money for part of the tuition and so it's pretty hard on her.

LEADER: What do you think your real chances are of meeting the picture you have of yourselves ten years from now? What do you think will really happen?

FIRST GIRL: I guess I'll become a teacher but I don't know about all the other things.

LEADER: What makes you think you'll make the teacher thing?

FIRST GIRL: Well, I guess because my mother's a teacher.

LEADER: Your mother's a teacher, so it seems very possible for you to go through those steps.

FIFTH BOY: Well, I think chances really aren't that great to become exactly what I want, because I've changed my mind so many times, and I'll probably change it again.

LEADER: But, no matter what you decide, what are the chances?

FIFTH BOY: You mean when I finally decide? I'd say they're good.

LEADER: How about you?

THIRD BOY: I really don't know. I think that, first of all, to get where I want to go, I'll have to be recognized by my school and be good in music.

LEADER: What do you think the chances are of your being recognized as good?

THIRD BOY: About 75 percent that I'll be recognized.

LEADER: And suppose they recognize you?

THIRD BOY: Then I'll be able to earn a living and have a family.

LEADER: What about your chances, your real chances?

SECOND GIRL: I really don't know. I'm not really sure about fashion design. I've changed my mind so many times that I'm running out of things to be.

LEADER: But, assuming that that was it. You didn't change your mind. What do you think are your chances of becoming a fashion designer? With all the things you have to go through to become one?

SECOND GIRL: Not very good.

LEADER: Why?

SECOND GIRL: Because I'm not really that good in art, and I know my parents would like me to go to college for things like math, history. I don't think they really want me to try anything like fashion designing. I've told them about it, and they didn't think too much of it.

LEADER: What did they want you to try?

SECOND GIRL: They really didn't give me any idea. I wanted to be a teacher, once. They liked that idea. I don't know.

LEADER: So what's making the chances difficult, the fact that your parents aren't agreeing to what you'd like to do, or your not being able to decide?

SECOND GIRL: Because of not being able to decide.

LEADER: But, do you think that regardless of what you come up with, the chances are good for you to make whatever it is? Do you have confidence about it?

SECOND GIRL: I guess pretty good. No, I don't really have confidence about it.

FIRST BOY: If I don't change again, then I think the chances are pretty good that I would become what I want to be. If I change again . . .

LEADER: What makes you think your chances are pretty good?

FIRST BOY: Well, I think that if you want to be something enough that you want to be it, then you have enough control over your life, at least I think I have enough control over my life to become what I want to be.

LEADER: What makes you think you have enough control over your life?

FIRST BOY: I don't know what really makes me think that, but nothing makes me think differently.

LEADER: Nothing makes you think that you don't have control. In other words, nobody put pressure on you too much, and whatever you decide you can fashion and shape without too much restriction.

FIRST BOY: Well, not so much with my family, but just with my own interests, what I want to continue thinking about or looking into, I would.

Evaluation

In many respects, the two groups were very similar. Each seemed aware of the possibilities for the future. Members of both groups voiced some misgivings and underwent changes of mind. A minority in each group seemed more or less confident than the others.

Many of the children in both groups hoped not to be married within the ten years that were projected. Whether this was a typical adolescent attitude, a product of parental influence, or simply due to a desire to have other experiences before making a commitment is not clear. Whatever the real reasons, the children seemed confident that this attitude could be rationally justified.

The girls in both groups were less specific or less sure of what they would be doing in ten years. This might have been a reflection of the culture's expectation that girls will be less specific about their plans for the future than boys. Neither the Upward Bound children nor the private-school children really addressed themselves to the subject of what they expected to be like as persons in ten years.

Perhaps the greatest similarity between the two groups was in the pervasive acceptance of a college education as a prerequisite for almost any vocation. Behind the apparent similarity, however, lies the greatest dissimilarity between the two groups. Whereas the private-school children expressed little doubt about the possibility of acting on their desire to go to college, the Hoboken children evinced little confidence that they would be able to also. The discrepancy between the ideal and the real was obviously much greater among the Upward Bound children than among the others.

Most of the Hoboken students recognized the financial and scholastic obstacles that had to be overcome and even seemed to know about possible sources of money, but they had no sound strategy for obtaining it. Selling a story, saving all one's earnings, and obtaining government financing are possible, but not probable, ways of getting money for college. Nor is attending a junior college realistic preparation for becoming a nuclear physicist, a writer, or a teacher.

The private-school children, on the other hand, seldom brought up the subject of money. They seemed to take for granted what is doubtlessly true, that money presented no stumbling block to them. Only one child made any reference to money. In contrast, many of the Hoboken children were very much concerned, not only about money for tuition, but about living comfortably in the suburbs, having a nice car, getting a good job (as "chief executive of a profit-making organization," for example). The need for money was also implied in their talk about possessions and travel.

The Hoboken students knew much less than the private-school students about the procedures for getting into college. Similarly, they had a less accurate conception of what college is like. The New York group chatted about high-school averages, college catalogues, entrance exams, interviews, the need to make a good impression, college acceptance, and the need to study and to experiment. They knew about the strong points of some colleges and the weaknesses of others and how one college might serve their needs better than another. They also understood that a bachelor's degree is not adequate for the attainment of some goals; they mentioned the master's degree and a teaching certificate as important, if not essential, to their future plans. They expressed interest in VISTA and the Peace Corps. The Hoboken students were not only unaware of such specifics but were misinformed about college and other subjects. The idea that college boards cannot be taken a second time, that nursing school is not difficult, that biology, chemistry, and algebra are the only prerequisites for nursing school are samples of such misinformation. In short, the Hoboken students had pieces of the puzzle, but these did not fit together.

The two groups expressed strikingly different reasons for wanting to go to college. Virtually every private-school student began with the statement, "I'm interested in . . . ." One student, interested in birds, planned to study ornithology; another, interested in history, planned to study history in order to teach it and enrich his travels throughout the world; a third, interested in music, planned to study music and play in an orchestra; a fourth, interested in fashion design, hoped to go to a school with a good program in that field. Except for the student who was interested in science and wanted to be a nuclear physicist (and that as a second choice), the Hoboken children did not base their reasons for going to college on any special interest. They would go to college because "it's better for you"; "your friends are still in school and you might as well go to college"; "it's a way of getting the things you want." Although the private-school students may have shared some of the pragmatic views of the Hoboken group, most of them seemed to be interested in preparing for a career they would enjoy, not just a job. What is more, this career would be based on any one of a wide variety of interests, whereas the Hoboken students, it seemed, could be satisfied only if they attained a single objective. This goal was unalterable—not subject to whimsical change. One of the private-school students, by contrast, mused: "Maybe I'll change my mind, but it'll be OK whatever I finally decide to be." The confidence evinced by such a child is undoubtedly the product of his economic stability.

The Hoboken students showed no inclination to emulate their parents. They did not want to feel trapped or tied down with a family in a city, without a good job and car, and without money. The private-school children, on the other hand, would not hesitate to follow in their parents' footsteps. They assumed that their lives would follow much the same pattern as their parents'. (When one youngster expressed the wish to continue living in the city, his peers nodded in agreement; another planned to be a teacher, like her mother.) In short, the private-school children benefited from having role models within the family, and the Hoboken children suffered for lack of them.

In summary, it can be said that the private-school children, as compared to the Hoboken children, have a great deal more specificity and awareness, base their possible future plans on their many varied interests, and seem to have found the strategies and role models for realizing their plans. While the Hoboken students have many pieces of an overall picture and do not feel altogether powerless, their statements about the possibilities for realizing their hopes for the future point sharply to some feelings of powerlessness in at least this area. The differences between the two groups can be deduced from the juxtaposition of statements below.

Upward Bound	*Private School*
"[My chances are] not very big. Unless the government will allow you to take out enough money to put you through."	"I'll become a teacher. . . . My mother's a teacher."
"With my marks, I don't even know if I'll get through high school."	"When I finally decide, I'll say they [the chances] are good."
"I'll have to get a job [for college] and whatever I make, I'll save it all . . . No, . . . when I see something I want, I'm going to spend it."	"To get where I want I'll have to be recognized by my school and be good in music. . . . [My chances are] about 75 percent that I'll be recognized." [The teacher verified this.]

"My chances are pretty bad. . . . My school marks are very bad. . . . It's shot."	"I think I have enough control over my life to become what I want to be. . . . Nothing makes me think differently."

As with other techniques for gathering information about groups of students, the question arises: How can the teacher utilize this feedback to develop more relevant lessons and units? There are a number of obvious possibilities.

SUGGESTED TEACHING PROCEDURES

One indicated project for the Hoboken children would be a visit to a nearby college. The teacher might arrange for the students to talk to professors, sit in on classes, and interview college students. In the interests of the many Upward Bound children who will probably not go to college for scholastic reasons, the teacher might initiate discussions in the area of vocational education. For the benefit of the many others whose chances of going to college are jeopardized by financial difficulties, a unit on "What Is Good Money?" might be developed in which they would investigate what "living comfortably" means, what they consider basic necessities, and what these cost.[6] Specialists in consumer education, even tax experts or financial advisors, might be recruited to lecture the group on budgeting, "forced saving," and other financial strategies. The students might undertake an extensive investigation of all the possible part-time or summer jobs—noting qualifications, hours, and pay—open to them within their immediate neighborhoods.

There are other less obvious but perhaps even more effective ways of utilizing the feedback. For example, prompted by the reluctance of the Hoboken students to emulate their parents, the teacher might raise the question, "In what ways

[6] An excellent unit on this subject, developed by Charles Rathbone and Stanley Litz, appears in *Urban Teacher Preparation Program* (Syracuse, N.Y.: Syracuse University, 1964–65).

would you like to be like your parents? In what ways would you like to be different from them?" This might introduce a discussion of desirable personality characteristics, offering the children an appreciation of positive traits in their own parents. While the unit need not be devoted to improving family relations, it does have the potential for making the students examine more closely some of the criteria they use for judging other people, especially those in their family. During such sessions the students might look into the possibilities for developing or eliminating some of the traits they uncover. Such an inquiry might lead to one on the subject of marriage, to which students from both groups made many references. What is a "good marriage" and how can it be achieved would be the indicated questions for discussion.

Another unit for the Hoboken students might be called "Controlling Your Future." For the many youngsters who lack know-how for realizing their objectives, a direct approach is often what is needed. Short-term exercises of two-to-five days' duration can help students to assess and improve their ability to make their wishes come true. The teacher might introduce such a unit with an exercise intended to help students realize a tertiary objective, such as talking to a certain person, reading a particular book, tasting yoghurt, playing tennis. Each student would articulate his objective; then the group would discuss how he might achieve it. At first the students would select goals that can be achieved within a week.[7] The rules for selecting an "action-program-of-the-week" should be simple: it should be fun, the student should have a high probability of bringing it to successful conclusion, it should contain elements of spontaneity. Sample action programs might revolve around statements like: "I'll finally ask ⎯⎯⎯⎯⎯ for a date," "I'll browse in that dress shop I've always wanted to go into," "I'll go out for the track team," or "I'll get my math homework in on time." Each student should record his progress on a personal chart. Throughout, the group should serve as a resource for analyzing the successes, failures, or difficulties encountered by in-

[7] This technique was suggested by Herbert A. Otto, op. cit., p. 2.

dividual students, making all the children responsible to one another. Subsequent action programs should be increasingly difficult and complex. Only after the students have tasted success should they embark on analysis of long-term goals.[8]

With such practical experience in making objectives come true, children like those from Hoboken can hope to approach the feeling of potency of the private-school student who declared, "I have enough control over my life to become what I want to be."

The feedback elicited from the private-school group was less suggestive of teaching techniques. Certainly, most of these children require no instruction for the attainment of feelings of power; their sense of potency is quite well developed. But some are not so sure of themselves. It is quite possible that the children who confessed to having had many changes of mind were not so comfortable with their situations as it might appear.

At least one more session would be required to determine whether this is indeed so and how best to approach these children. It can be tentatively suggested, however, that the confident children might become even more so if they were prompted to help the less sure children realize some of their plans. In so doing, they would develop their own sense of power *with* another person rather than *over*, while helping this other person become more sure of himself.

"TIME CAPSULE"

A third technique for learning more about groups of students revolves around the preparation of a "time capsule." This method is designed primarily to furnish information about how children define themselves and what they use for criteria, but it can elicit cues to all three concerns which can contribute to the development of useful materials. To test

[8] For an excellent resource, see materials developed by A. Alschuler *et al.*, of the Achievement Motivation Development Project, and published by Education Ventures, Inc., Middletown, Conn.

the effectiveness of the technique, teachers of four classes in three cities used it in the following manner.

Each teacher described a time capsule, telling the class about the one deposited at the New York World's Fair of 1939–40 or about the capsules found in Egyptian tombs and in the graves of American Indians. The teacher emphasized the fact that careful preservation of artifacts and writings make it possible for one generation of people to become informed about another generation long since passed away and pointed out that the invention of records, especially taped records, has made it possible for our own civilization to lay away much more information for the enlightenment of future generations than did any civilization in the past.

The students were then invited to prepare a time capsule about their class to inform a man of the future, a thousand years from now, what the people in the class were like. The capsule was to contain three examples of song lyrics, pictures from magazines, and ten- to fifteen-minute tape recordings by the students. Since there was to be only one time capsule for the entire class, each student was encouraged to contribute ideas. All suggestions were listed on the board and the class chose among them after debate and discussion. Student comments during the process of decision-making and the criteria for including or excluding data were recorded.

The "Time Capsule" technique was tried in four schools: two high-school classes in East Orange, New Jersey, one made up predominantly of Negro students of average academic ability, the other composed for the most part of college-bound, middle-class white students; a sixth-grade class of Negro students in New Orleans whose teacher thought of them as "an average group"; and a fairly well-integrated elementary classroom in Racine, Wisconsin, with children of upper-lower-class background. Field-group members Joseph Bongo and Martin Haberman reported from East Orange and Racine, respectively. Field-group members Emma and Stanton Plattor reported from New Orleans.

Since some of the cooperating teachers were reluctant to spend more than two or three days on the time capsule, not all of them completed the assignment. The teacher in Racine dropped the experiment after a short time because his students were not interested in preparing it and did not want to talk about themselves. The other teachers, however, reported that their classes were enthusiastic about working on the time capsule. As will be seen, some reports were more elaborate than others.

For the reasons given, the Racine report was a particularly sketchy one. Selections were as follows:

Songs
    "The Battle Hymn of the Republic"
    "The Star Spangled Banner"
    "Whoa Mule Whoa"

Pictures
    A very elaborately frosted pink and white birthday cake
    A grassy field with trees in the background
    A formal garden with clipped boxwood, walkways, and other shrubs and flowers

There was no tape recording. The children decided to deposit newspaper articles in the time capsule instead. (In general, these children were reluctant to talk about themselves, preferring to discuss their interests.) Their clippings included: "Dear Abby" columns, articles about family problems and divorce, and how-to-be-pretty articles.

The East Orange Negro students made the following selections:

Songs
    "The Impossible Dream," from *Man of La Mancha*
    "Blowin' in the Wind," by Bob Dylan

Pictures
    The New York City skyline
    Negroes rioting
    Negro and white soldiers in Vietnam
    A photograph of the class as a group standing in front of the school

Tape Recording

Instead of taping comments that would be most revealing about the nature of the class, these students taped predictions and questions about the future. Virtually every student said something to the effect that the world is "in a mess," but that with a lot of effort "things could be better in the future." A few students predicted total war and the end of the world.

The other high-school class in East Orange, mostly middle class and white, did not select songs and pictures for inclusion in the capsule. They discussed only what to record on tape. They wanted the tape to include the following types of statements (paraphrased by their teacher):

We have all kinds of pressures.

People are always telling us what to do.

We have to take courses that have no meaning to us.

Adults tell us to decide, and then they don't like the decisions.

We're not all the same—there are different points of view among us.

We want to move without too many restrictions.

We want to become more aware of things by ourselves.

We want to shape our own lives.

Even though things are complicated, we're still enthusiastic.

Adults want us to conform, and so we lose our identity.

We have to conform to the group, so our friends will like us.

You have to have good grades to be somebody.

The most comprehensive report came from the New Orleans sixth-graders.

Songs

Because there was considerable disagreement in selecting the three songs that were required of them, it was decided to include all the original suggestions. Many of these were annotated by their protagonists. Asterisks denote the two songs that finally seemed most applicable.

"Soldier Boy" ("about a boy in the Army—has a girl-friend here")

"Reveille" ("you can't get him up—like me, I'm lazy")

"John Henry" ("a man like steel—no one could hardly hurt him")

*"Greetings, This Is Uncle Sam" ("drafting boys for the army")

"America"

"Dedicated to the Greatest" ("about somebody who dies and he's famous and we show our gratitude")

"Love Is a Hurting Thing" ("about someone in the army, and he gets married and then has to go back into the army")

"The Day They Took the Old Folks Away"

"If I Had a Hammer" ("tells how much you love your brothers and sisters")

*"You Can't Hurry Love"

"Working in the Coal Mine" ("tells how people in the country live")

"Breaking My Back Instead of Using My Mind" ("this isn't what *we're* like")

Pictures

The children decided to draw their own pictures rather than cut them out of magazines. They made drawings of

A church ("because everybody should go and worship and that's what we do")

A city ("to show how people live in these days")

Vietnam ("because boys are over there trying to protect us")

Tape Recording

The children did not make a final decision about what should be on the tape. But they made a number of suggestions:

"We should tell about holidays we celebrate."

"We could tell about things at school—like the music program."

"Museums—they'd tell a lot."

"Tell about animals of the world."

The teacher then asked the class: "Have you said anything that's pertinent to you as Negroes? Should people digging up the capsule know something specific about how Negroes live in the United States?" This provoked some lively rejoinders which revealed that, in the eyes of the children, any number of subjects would illuminate their status as Negroes.

We have Democrats and Republicans. As the Republican people came in, the Negroes became free, and with President Kennedy they became free and could run for office and get more education. The more Democrats come in, the weaker the Negroes grow.

The Democrats call some of us Negroes stupid because of some of the riots they have in California. They are mostly Negroes starting those riots. I think if some of us would stop those riots maybe we could get friends with the Democrats.

The Negroes and the whites should be free, but part of Russia is part of China, and they have yellow people, and I don't know who they are, but the Chinese are yellow. And if the yellow Chinese and us Negroes and the whites joined together we could live together and no fighting, and we could probably have a better life together.

The time capsule activity prompted an exhaustive dialogue between teacher and students in New Orleans.

TEACHER: What would you tell other people in the future about what we are like?

STUDENTS:—Television, electricity—things we have made or done.

　　　　—Samples of clothes and of animals.
　　　　—Tape recorders and automobiles.
　　　　—Samples of schools and homes.
　　　　—Samples of modern home appliances.
　TEACHER: How would we tell what we personally are
like? What kind of people we are? How we feel?
　STUDENTS:—By writing a book about our life.
　　　　—By telling how we live, the things we use
to fix food.
　　　　—With leaves and trees.
　　　　—By drawing people going to work.
　　　　—By giving samples of churches.
　　　　—By leading tools, weapons, dishes, recipes.
　TEACHER: If you were going to tell people about you,
you'd have to tell them how you feel.
　STUDENTS:—Like if you have no shoes and no clothing,
you're sad.
　　　　—You feel worried when someone is lost,
and you can't find him, and you worry if he's safe or
something.
　　　　—You worry when your father's away on a
camping trip and is supposed to stay for a short time, and
he doesn't come home.
　　　　—And when your son's in Vietnam and
doesn't write.
　　　　—Like you worry if your aunt says she's
gonna pick you up for the summer vacation, and she
doesn't come.
　　　　—Like you cry for sad when you lose some-
one in your family.
　　　　—When you and a friend have a fight and
try to make up and can't, you feel sorry.
　TEACHER: What are you worrying about right now?
　STUDENTS:—Passing to seventh grade.
　　　　—Grades.
　　　　—Being a high-school student.
　　　　—Getting a job.
　　　　—Feeling afraid.

Evaluation

Within the limitations described below, the feedback yielded by the "Time Capsule" technique can be quite useful. Rather vague patterns of concern can be inferred from the experiments with the technique. Some of the children's statements seem to reflect a concern for self-identity, as in the references to the need for good grades in order "to be somebody," or the identification with the song "John Henry," or, indeed, the reluctance of the Racine children to talk about themselves. It is possible, too, that both the elegant, out-of-reach pictures selected by the Racine group and the lyrics of "Blowin' in the Wind," selected by the East Orange Negro children, indicate a sense of being cut off, a sense of powerlessness, a concern for connectedness. The statements by the white children in East Orange about always being told "what to do," about "too many restrictions," and about their desire to "shape our own lives" seem to indicate a concern for power. It may also be that the many expressions of fear of loss and separation by the New Orleans children reflect the three concerns under consideration. Yet these interpretations are at best nebulous and indefinite. Not enough evidence was gathered from the applications of the technique to confirm the accuracy of such interpretations.

Feedback from the Time Capsule technique then, is, in some respects, limited. Very few direct, full statements, reflective of the children's concerns (such as the cues listed in the model), were recorded in any of the experiments. Moreover, even when a concern can be inferred from the feedback, such as the concern for connectedness evident in the numerous references to war, separation, divorce, or being left alone, it is not clear how the children deal with the particular concern. Besides, it is difficult to tell when the children are saying what they think they should be saying and when they are really revealing their feelings. For example, do the patriotic songs, the idealistic lyrics of the "Impossible Dream," and the pictures of the church, with which some of the children identified, really represent them, or do they represent their desire to be associated with accepted values? In brief, the technique itself raises questions about the validity of equating the children's selections with their true concerns.

Suggested Teaching Procedures

Because of the limited value of the information it yields, the Time Capsule technique is only the first step in discovering how children feel about themselves and how they deal with their concerns. But it does lead to a second step which can be very fruitful: probing selections themselves. Having uncovered "The Impossible Dream" as the song that his group of children regard as most revealing of themselves, the teacher might have the children dissect the song to determine the meaning for them of an "unbeatable foe" and an "unrightable wrong." Similarly, he might probe their avowed preference for New York City, asking, "What is there about you that makes you pick New York City, rather than a smaller city or town? Why is New York City most representative of you?" Utilizing the "Dear Abby" selection, he might ask the children, "What would you write to Abby about this class?" He might then set up a committee of little Abbys to answer the letter that emerged. Or he might have the children analyze Abby—figure out what kind of friend, mother, teacher, neighbor, she would be. Such ramifications of the original selections might elicit further cues that begin to uncover how the children deal with their concerns.

Taking the feedback at face value suggests a number of other immediate, relevant, often affective uses. For example, the teacher might accept the Racine children's interest in newspaper articles about family problems and divorce as a signal to talk more directly about families: "What is a family?" he might ask his students. Or "Can there be a family if the mother or father is not present? What are the different ways in which you can act in a family?" The East Orange and New Orleans selections having to do with war and Vietnam might indicate a desire on the part of the children to know more about war—a topic that is rarely discussed, particularly in elementary schools. Selections representing a fear of instability, loss, and separation might suggest the appropriateness of a series of lessons or a unit dealing with change and impermanence. Indeed, much of the traditional curriculum could be presented in terms of change: westward expansion could be taught in a way that emphasizes the feelings people have about leaving friends behind and learning new ways of living; literature could be examined in the light of the characters' reactions to change; science lessons could be applied to personal and social change, impermanence, evolution, and the consequences of disturbing the ecological niche of an organism. In short, taking the feedback at face value suggests not only new areas for instruction but also ideas for reorganization of the mandatory school curriculum in terms of such concerns as change, family, war, and so on.

The feedback suggests other teaching possibilities, as well. The very jumbled comments of the New Orleans children about Democrats, Republicans, Russia, and China should alert their teacher to do something to correct their misconceptions. The New Orleans and East Orange children's worries about grades might serve to introduce a series of lessons on how people evaluate themselves. The desired outcomes from the children after such lessons might be such statements as "I'm going to try to get good grades, but I know they're not everything" or "Good grades may be only one aspect of being someone special." Racine's "how-to-be-pretty" selection offers wonderful affective teaching possibilities for children who show reluctance to talk about themselves. The teacher could set up a role-playing situation in which teams of one boy and one girl play the parents of an ugly child, telling what they would say or do to help the child be happy in our society. The teacher might play the part of the child and decide which parents have been the most helpful to him.

In summary, although the Time Capsule technique as designed did not elicit as many cues to how children deal with their concerns (especially self-identity) as we had hoped, it did suggest additional areas to probe for cues and possible topics for affective lessons. While the technique can be used profitably in its present form, it may be preferable to vary certain facets of it. For example, more cues to concerns might be elicited if the teacher allowed each student to make his own time capsule. From a composite of the individual capsules prepared, he might be able to extract and analyze common patterns of concern of the group as a whole.

6

INTEGRATING CONCERNS, THOUGHT, AND ACTION: "THE TRUMPET"

As the model was applied and reapplied and diagnostic techniques were refined, it became apparent that a strategy for sequencing content and procedure would be necessary if experiments with the model were to be widely reproduced. Toward this end, the field group developed a pictorial representation of just such a strategy, which we called the "trumpet" (pictured on p. 164).

According to this approach to sequencing, any lesson or series of techniques employed should allow the learner to engage in the processes itemized below. Each of these processes, as well as each level of dealing with the three basic concerns of connectedness, self-identity, and potency (shown at the mouth of the trumpet), is represented by an archetypal question or statement.

—Inventory—How do I respond?

—Distinguish—How do others respond?

—Determine assumptions—Why do I (they) respond that way?

—Describe consequences—What happens because of certain responses?

—Try on other sets—What is it like when I respond this way or that way?

—Choose for longer-term experimentation—Of these responses, which one do I want for this time and for this situation?

During the summer of 1967, the trumpet was adapted and refined for use in the Philadelphia Cooperative School Program, a program for an extremely diverse group of city children from grades 4 to 12. In the following report, Terry Borton, director of the program, explains his interpretation of the trumpet and his adaptation of it to the Philadelphia program.[1]

The trumpet was developed by a national group of educators in an attempt to find a curriculum that was more relevant to the basic psychological concerns of children than others in current use. It seemed to us that each individual's development (represented on the trumpet by the nautilus-shaped spiral at left) was influenced by the interaction between his environment and the three basic concerns of connectedness, self-identity, and potency.

Our problem was to find a method of describing the process through which people move from simple awareness of these concerns to conscious action based on an understanding of their feelings. What we did in the trumpet was to focus on an aspect of the individual's development—it might be long hair, a love affair, or a friendship—and examine the process by which the individual moves from a reaction based on emotion alone to a response based on information plus emotion. This process, the integration of concerns, thought,

[1] The following account is copyright © 1970 by Terry Borton. Reprinted by permission.

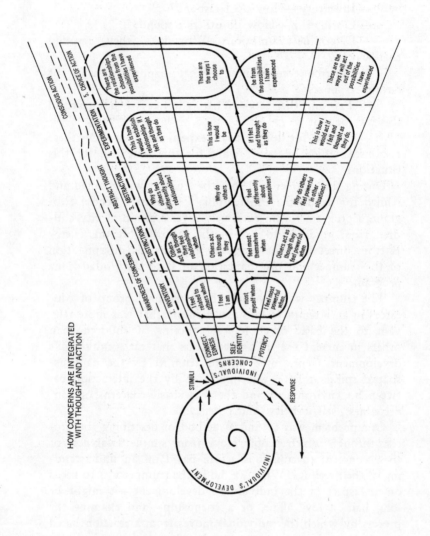

HOW CONCERNS ARE INTEGRATED
WITH THOUGHT AND ACTION

CONSCIOUS ACTION

5. CHOICE OF ACTION

These are the relationships I choose from the possibilities I have experienced

These are the ways I choose to

be from the possibilities I have experienced

These are the ways I will act out of the possibilities I have experienced

4. EXPERIMENTATION

This is how I would establish if I relationships thought felt and thought as they do

This is how I would be

if I felt and thought as they do

This is how I would act if I felt and thought as they do

ABSTRACT THOUGHT

3. ABSTRACTION

Why do others feel differently about relationships?

Why do others

feel differently about themselves?

Why do others feel powerful in other situations?

AWARENESS OF CONCERNS

2. DISTINCTIONS

Others act as though they feel relationships when

Others act as though they

feel most themselves when

Others act as though they feel powerful when

1. INVENTORY

I feel related to others when

I feel I am

most myself when

I feel most powerful when

CONNECT-EDNESS

SELF-IDENTITY

POTENCY

INDIVIDUAL'S CONCERNS

STIMULI

RESPONSE

INDIVIDUAL'S DEVELOPMENT

and action, might be instantaneous or it might occur over a lifetime. It might be partially completed; it might focus on a major incident or a minor one; it might wander through a thousand personal idiosyncrasies. But we felt that unless we could find some pattern of development, we would never be able to develop a curriculum that would help students to understand the most important part of themselves. We would be forced to rely on the psychiatrist's couch, at one extreme, or, at the other, on the vague hope that English classes would somehow teach what it means to be human between gerund clauses and major British authors.

The trumpet depicts the process of personal integration as having three phases in each of which a different function assumes the most important role—*awareness of concerns, abstract thought,* and *conscious action* (the flowing lines at the head of the chart). Within these functions the development of a concern is represented by generic questions or statements. At the "inventory" level, for example, one can survey one's feelings about identity by completing the statement, "I feel I am most myself when . . ." or "I am a person who . . . ."

To teach the process of personal integration requires a curriculum (represented by the figure-8 lines) that interweaves the three concerns with awareness, abstract thought, and conscious action. The curricular materials I used as an example here are an attempt to begin teaching the process at the five-year-old level. They provide a way for the parent or teacher to speak directly to the connectedness, self-identity, and potency of a five-year-old. Four books were produced, with a total vocabulary of only twenty-five words—so few that a child who knows what words are can begin to sight-read the books with very little effort. The pictures are the work of my daughter, Lynn, who was six years old at the time.

INVENTORY: "I AM A DOG FOR YOU"

Book One contains only eight words. Yet those eight words manage to explore the first level of awareness, an *inventory* of feelings focused around the general relationship between

BOOK I

child and dog. The teacher can use the child's actions in reading—his bowing up and down, or bow-wowing at the top of his lungs—to explore his concerns as they are focused around his relationship with this mythical dog. Through word play, the connectedness ("I am a bow-wow dog for you") is firmly established. So is the dog's identity ("I am a bow-wow dog"). The child's identity is recognized by the fact that the book speaks directly to him ("I bow-wow for you"). The book is full of potency (You bow—wow!—*bow wow!*). But because the dog is imaginary and funny-looking—not big and real and fierce—these concerns are likely to be expressed positively, and the teacher can easily make the child consciously aware of his feelings.

In Book One the inventory of concerns is performed only indirectly, by making the child aware of how he is responding. A more direct approach would be to ask the child such generic questions as "What do you feel about this dog?" or, at a later stage of development, "What do you feel about your hair?" "About your love affair?"

DISTINCTIONS: "ARE YOU A DOG?"

Book Two corresponds to the level of the trumpet at which the child begins to make *distinctions* between the way he acts because of his feelings and the way others (in this case the dog) act on the basis of their's. In Book Two this level is explored by discussing a distinction:

ARE YOU A DOG?   (Child answers, "No.")
CAN YOU BOW-WOW? (Child's answer makes no difference.)
BOW WOW!   (Child bow-wows.)
YOU *CAN* BOW-WOW. (Child is caught.)

Once this distinction is dispensed with, the book concludes:

WOW!
YOU *ARE* A DOG!

BOOK II

The child knows this is not true. And just to make sure:

NO! NO! NO!
YOU ARE *YOU!*

The point is not to make the child think he is a dog but to raise in a humorous way the question of the difference between child and dog if both do the same thing. Because a dog is not a person, this question of self-identity cannot be pushed very far, nor need it be. There should be plenty of other opportunities built into school curricula for students to make distinctions between the way they feel and the way others feel, so that they can explore other possibilities such as "Others act as though they feel most themselves when . . . they are kicking dogs . . . or wearing long hair . . . or drinking with a pretty stranger at a cocktail party."

ABSTRACTION: "WHY DOES DOG LIKE YOU?"

Book Three corresponds to the third level of the trumpet, the level at which abstract thought changes simple awareness into a generalized understanding of the assumptions that underlie the difference in the way people feel and act. The key question for each concern is "Why?"

DOG IS NOT LIKE YOU.
    WHY DO YOU LIKE DOG?
YOU ARE NOT LIKE DOG.
    WHY DOES DOG LIKE YOU?

The answers the children give vary tremendously, although often it is, "I dunno." Often, too, the child seems a little puzzled about why anyone should raise the question—the same child who at age three drove his family crazy by continually asking "Why?" Although the trumpet does not correspond to any chronological development, most mothers can attest that this phase is typical of three-year-olds. The same phenomenon occurs again, so the folklore has it, during

BOOK III

the sophomore year of college. That is the second major time in his life when a person realizes that others whom he respects are operating on values different from his. But for much of our lives there is little opportunity for experiences which encourage us to question directly our own value assumptions and those of other people. Why?

EXPERIMENTATION: "YOU CAN BE DOG"

In order to answer the "Why?" questions raised at level 3, Book Four suggests that "You Can Be Dog" by acting the way the dog acts and feeling as the dog feels.

YOU CAN BOW-WOW.
YOU CAN PANT-PANT.
YOU CAN LIKE DOGS.
YOU CAN LIKE YOU.

As in Book One, reading the lines should provide a means for the child to experience what it might be like to be a dog. One little girl panted and hugged herself when she read "You can like you." She was playing at being dog the way children play at being elephant, doctor, mother, or trashman. But in Book Four, the child can be taught that play, or the natural process of experimenting with how others act and feel, can be used as a conscious technique to broaden the possibilities of our own understanding.

For the child, such improvisation is easy. He can play at many things and be held responsible for relatively few. As he gets older, he is not only required to play "the game of life" in deadly earnest but the opportunities in which he can play without consequences disappear. Where in our society can an adult experiment with new means of relating to people, or of being, or of using power, without suffering severe reprisals if he makes a mistake? Where can he learn roles that might be more appropriate for today's social and moral turmoil than the ones he learned as a three-year-old or as a teenager?

If you are not like dog and dog is not like you	Why does dog like you!	Why? ?	You can be dog!
You can bow-wow.	You can pant-pant.	You can like dogs.	You can like you.
Wow!	You can be dog and you can be you.	You can see why dog likes you.	Dog likes you if
You like dog	AND YOU LIKE YOU.	Bow Wow!	

BOOK IV

The last few pages of Book Four moralize their way through the complications of level 5, Choice of Action.

DOG LIKES YOU IF
YOU LIKE DOG
AND YOU LIKE YOU.

Level 5 describes a choice of action based on personal *experimentation* with other people's ways of expressing connectedness, self-identity, and potency. The choice may be the same path the individual has always taken, perhaps for new reasons, or it may be so radical a departure from his previous actions that it brings violent consequences. Whatever the choice of action, even if it is no action, there will be consequences of some sort, which lead to a reevaluation of the choice and a beginning of the whole process all over again, with new awareness, new thought, and new action.

Once we understand the integrating process, even in the crude form represented in the foregoing schema, it becomes easier to understand what is happening in the confusing maelstrom of personalities and activities which envelop us. The trumpet is a process chart, not a report card. Yet it is possible to see that some people have come to depend primarily on one process and therefore never seem to be able to do what they want to do. Even those who understand the process of integration vary widely in what they do with it. Some limit themselves to their little problems and end their lives as little men. Some tackle their great problems, and, while they do not necessarily have all the answers, they have a direction and purpose in their lives.

If one of the aims of education is to produce more people who have conscious control of themselves and so are able to function effectively in a world of rapid social and moral change, then we must find many kinds of curricula that can be used to develop these traits—curricula that can be used in a school setting by ordinary teachers. The BOW WOW series is one example. The sensitivity-training groups sponsored by the National Training Laboratories are also excellent devices because they abolish the usual role expectations and provide for instant feedback of other people's feelings. Books like *Improvisation for the Theatre*, by Viola Spolin,[1] provide specific lesson plans for teaching students how to express new ways of feeling and thinking in new forms of personal action.

[1] (Evanston, Ill.: Northwestern University Press, 1963).

7

GAMES

Among the techniques devised for implementing the model are certain "games" that involve the self and the affective realm. As distinct from the many games that have been constructed along subject-matter lines, we looked for a procedure that would cut across subject-matter boundaries and engage the whole area of feeling and affect. We asked the Western Behavioral Sciences Institute (WBSI), of La Jolla, California, which had previous experience in constructing games for business, industry, and education personnel, to develop, test, and evaluate a pilot game or game-like procedure that classroom teachers could use to help students expand their views of self and increase self-esteem. The following material is adapted from WBSI's final report to us, as summarized by Hall T. Sprague, a Program Associate.

During May and June, the director read and thought about "self-concept" and related topics, consulted with WBSI staff members, staged a staff "brainstorming" session, and roughed out several ideas for self-concept games and exercises. These "ideas" are presented in five categories: (1) constraints—some of the limits within which any products of our work would have to fit; (2) goals—some outcomes that might be sought; (3) concepts, derived from reading, that might be represented or dealt with in a self-concept game; (4) events or activities that might be part of games; and (5) props that might be employed in games. About a month before the first meeting with students we defined the assignment this way:

> Within the constraints, and moving in the direction of the goals, design some games in which certain concepts, represented by things or by players acting out certain episodes, are brought home to the players in order to help them increase their self-esteem.

Twenty youngsters, aged seven through ten were recruited from a Negro neighborhood in southeast San Diego. If the children had any expectations about our meetings they were that the meetings would be a sort of day camp "extension." Last-minute preparations for the meetings with the children included the purchase of "supplies" at toy stores, display stores, and discount houses, the development of a general format for the first two days, and brief rehearsals and equipment checks.

From July 3 to July 28, we met with the kids from about 9:30 to 12:00 each weekday morning, in a total of nineteen meetings. Our staff group numbered two to five each day, and a total of seven different WBSI staff members or volunteers participated in the meetings. The number of children present each day ranged between eight and twenty-one; about ten of the kids were "regulars," and about fifteen were "near-regulars." Before and after the meetings, the staff discussed the day's events, evaluated progress, revised goals as necessary, recorded impressions, and planned the next day's meeting.

Here are samples of the ideas developed at brainstorming sessions: The ideas are presented in sketchy form, just as they emerged at the sessions.

Constraints

Teacher is the user
4–6 weeks of class time
Verbal, active, and simple
Small steps
Much feedback between steps
Much help needed on branching and improvising
Usable in a classroom
By August 1
Not used to dialogue (monologue)
Relatively nonverbal

Goals

Give the kids chances to be rewarders
Give the kids experiences with and insights into self-concept change
Show them that self-concept can change
Give them a chance to turn their current thoughts and feelings immediately into action
Help them know and feel that sometimes they like themselves, sometimes they don't
Teach them that there is an "I" each person would like to be, an ideal self
Teach them that each child is different from what he used to be and will be different later on
Have kids see themselves as planning, purposive, choosing, individual, responsible, accountable
Have each kid construct an environment in which the best "I" could operate
Have each kid describe a worst self
Have each kid describe what criteria he uses to judge his worst self

Have each child describe an environment that is worst for him (for all)

Have the child find out that others see him as having certain characteristics

Have him know that he would like to be different in some ways

Help each child discover and use some strengths that he didn't know he had and that he can call on in the future

Give the kids chances to control other kids

Enable them to gain self-regard

Preparation for the first meeting with the children included drawing up lists of day-by-day objectives.

1) Series of activities to: Get acquainted
                                  Get in the game spirit
                                  Get kids used to being paid attention to
                                  Build group membership

So that kids want to be there.

2) Series of activities to: Get each kid to experience and gain insight into his distinctiveness as a person

     So that they   "see" that they are someone unique and how they get that way.

3) Series of activities to: Give each kid some control experiences
                                    Give each kid some acceptance experiences

     So that they   feel muscles they didn't know they had and that they can count on in the future.

4) Series of activities to: Allow kids to talk about or make experience—insight, connections regarding self-concept and performance

So that they   become more self-aware.

5) Some time for closure and "keys" to return to the "authentic" classroom again

So that this does not become an isolated experience and so that they have a way of building on the experience.

Concepts

The difference between what is me and what is mine
Self equals all that I can call mine:

Material = body, clothes, parents, children, house, possessions

Social = others' images, ways of being with others, my investment in others, roles

Spiritual = presider over perceptions; comparer and producer of self-love or self-hate

My hunch about how you see me
Sense of personal identity—based on some continuity of "me" over time and from one situation to another

One's self exists only insofar as the selves of others exist
Good me, bad me, not me
The I that I use
The I that is in me but isn't available
The I that I use most
Things I recognize as characteristic of me
Each self or type of self or part of self has certain physical characteristics and skills and traits

Events and Activities

Play with dummies of family members
Make up a play, act it out
Take away kid's self with a big bag
Do things as a group that one person can't do, . . . like lifting a heavy object
Control the environment with lights, sounds

Make up faces from police identification kit

Make a mask that looks like you; make one that looks as you would like to look

Let the kids "blow up," vent their explosive feelings . . . then reconstruct

Kids keep a big name tag on which are written all the good things they have learned about themselves

Kids choose masks for mother, father, sibling, teacher dummies

Kids pick their mood by putting on a mask or a sign

Kids get rewards for themselves which they take home

Kids look in mirror and describe themselves. Look in mirror and tell two good things about yourself (say them to yourself aloud, in front of the group)

Look in mirror at yourself with other kids saying good things they think about you

Kids help "Mr. C," a man of limited capacities, learn about them

Kids make up a "Mr. C," give him capacities so that he will understand them

Kids help "Mr. O" make up a kid that would be a neat kid

Kids make up a kid that "Mr. O," given his peculiar tastes, would choose

Kids design a school that would help "Mr. L" to know more that matters

Kids tell amnesia victim how things are, what they are like

Make a mask that looks like you feel when you've . . . .

Choose masks that illustrate your mood today or your self-concept

Make masks for yourself . . . for your various selves

Make masks for other kids

Kid gives himself a new name, a new identity . . . acts like that person, who could be an ideal me, a possible me, an irresponsible me

Sort cards describing acts into good-me, bad-me, not-me piles

Kids take turns filling in the character of a dummy . . .
or filling in the end of a story about him

Each kid talks about how photos of people and animals
are like him

Kids have access at all time to big signs with arrows
which they can use to express feelings "I hate you," "I need
you," "Feeling great today," "Really afraid today"

Kid discusses himself as a companion for himself

Adults serve as aides to help kids do what they want to
do. Kids are given choices about what to do, adults sit in
center. Students "sign up" to get adults to help them.

Props

    Mirror
    Mask
    Cardboard box
    "Mr. A" figure
    Dummy
    Telephone
    Carnival funny-photo stand
    Cards that describe a person
    Paper money
    Photos of people and animals
    A big hollow figure into which a kid can put himself
    Paper-bag masks
    Name cards or badges
    Huge bag that fits over kids
    Huge things that require more than one person to lift
them
    Radio
    Light-show materials
    "We-are-special" sign
    Paper costumes
    Police identification kit
    Overhead projector
    Rear-screen projector
    Polaroid camera
    Diploma
    Musical instruments

Rhythm makers
Shapes—jagged, rough, smooth
Colors
Clay
Xerox machine
Military-type insignia
Travel tickets
Neutral objects, like a brick
Squirt gun
Lifesize puppet
Success-rigged slot machine
Comb and mirror

The games selected for presentation here inquire directly into children's feelings.

"COMPLAIN, GRIPE, AND MOAN"

Each child is given three coupons, tickets, or pieces of paper money. On one the word "Home" is written; on the others, "School" and "Block." Adults (or other children) sit in three booths marked "Home," "School," and "Block." The children go to each booth and spend their coupon to complain about what's wrong at home, at school, or on the block (in the neighborhood). The booth occupants record the complaints.

Comments

The kids seemed different when they came into the booths to complain: more serious, more straight (some), more cogitative. Most of them were pretty interested in the game and most of them used all their coupons. The game needs something to keep the kids busy when they're not complaining.

Our general impression was that we were hearing real, if very incomplete, portrayals of what bothers these kids, and the game's main function, legitimizing griping, may be a good idea. The complaints made by the kids, listed below, were used as data for later games and teaching experiences.

On the Block

Too many fights on the corner—people that live down there

Kids are bad—teenagers hit me

Kids try to make me fight—tell me to hit another kid —tell another kid to hit me

Can't like it when they fight my best friends

Sometimes I get beat up

Nobody to play with on the street

Coming from school, kids throw rocks and hit me

Too quiet

Mortuary is too close

Never have fun when I go somewhere

Sometimes there are no children

Only about three or two kids on my block

I don't like to stay in the yard all the time and watch my little sister—she's bad

When we catch a pigeon in the park they won't let us keep it

When we hit a window accidentally, they get mad

Guys always mess up our storehouse at home

They start fires in the weeds—teenagers

Me and my sister are always fighting at the block

My next-door neighbor fights

Nobody hardly to play with, and my best friend is fixing to move

Some kids I can't play with, because my mother fights with their mothers

At Home

Doesn't like church every night

Brothers spoiled—takes their stuff and then hits them if they come home late

Icebox raids are discouraged

Brothers and sisters hit her

Whipped sometimes, but softly

Mother wants her to come back on time—comes back too early, then comes back too late

Teenagers fight

Too many cars on Sunday—man got shot, happens every Sunday, wants to move away from park because men fight

Nothing to do around home, nobody to play with around home

Whips me, can't go outside

No friends, nobody to play with

Whacks brother, mother whips her

Brother broke seahorse soap

Doesn't get to sit by window in station wagon

Nothing to do

Washes dishes, goes to store—brother never does—never gets a penny

Doesn't like going to park on Sunday

Has to go to church every day

Fights with nine-year-old

Nothing to do, plays with dog sometimes

Father makes him work, weed garden

Doesn't like brother because he teases—kicks him in leg, gets beat up for it

Mom screams because she fights with sister

School lesson—he gets mad, hates school

In School

Teacher is mean

Teacher is always telling us not to play games

When one strays out of area, send us back to room

Teacher always screams at her

Too many fights (kids)

Teacher gives hard work

They don't let you run around in the playground

Kids trying to pick fights beat you up for something

Hit you with balls, name calling

Too many fibs on you—kids

Gets whippings for nothing

Don't get to play record player

Paddles you for going outside

Teacher sends her to office for nothing

Four papers in one day

Teacher pulls ears—feels like she's pulling gum

Chokes you by neck

Laughs at you in the office (when ready to see principal)

Teacher is mean—makes you wash mouth out with soap. Brought vinegar and soap and made them wash mouth out with soap

Kids are smarty-pants

Girls beat up on boys—sixth-grade girls and younger boys

Make arithmetic easier

More recess

Have to stay after school to finish things—sometimes have to finish in office

Stay after school, write "I will behave" fifty times

Teacher pinches on shoulder with fingernails—hurts a lot

Teacher tells him to stand on one leg if he talks, and if he puts leg down, she hits him with long round stick

People tell fibs on each other

VARIATIONS OF "COMPLAIN, GRIPE, AND MOAN"

Each player gets four chits: "School," "Block," "Home," "Me." Instead of complaining, they tell things they would like to have in the home, school, block, and for themselves. The interviewers record remarks and ask questions in case certain topics aren't covered fully. The questions asked by the recorders in each booth were as follows:

School. "What are some things you would like to learn or know how to do?"

Home. "If you could add someone to live in your house, what kind of person would you choose?"

Block. "What if a new park were added in your neighborhood—what would you want to be in it?"

Me. "What are some things you would like to have for yourself?"

Comments

The game did not engage the children as the original had. We should have tried a variation called "Remedy," in which we asked them for ways to improve the things they complained about in the first game.

Some of their comments were surprising. Lydia, who seems unscholarly, isn't anti-book, but she is against difficult books. One of the things she wanted in school was more books, ones that she can read. Daryl, who seems bright, wanted older kids running the school as teachers and principal, and he had other ideas for making school a better place. Many wanted more siblings and friends. We had little success in getting the kids to talk about personal qualities or achievements they would like, rather than toys. Donna (a big thinker) wanted to own a restaurant.

The main virtue of the exercise, as with "Complain," may be that it offers a way to learn something about the kids' world; it takes their view of things seriously, and it allows them to lead a conversation with adults.

This variation might have been more successful had some of the questions been reworded to stress personal characteristics or feelings rather than things or possessions. "What would you like to have happen to you at home, at school, in the neighborhood?" or "What are some ways you might like people to act or be?" might be rewarding questions.

In another variation each station would be a situational booth in which the children would respond to different situations. Any of the following situations might be described to the children at one or another booth.

School. "A new school is to be built and the people of this city want it to be the best ever. They've asked a lot of questions, talked with many teachers, and visited many schools, but they think kids know more about schools than anyone else. So they're asking you to help them. Tell me, what do you think the best school would be like, look like, what you'd do there, who'd be there, what you'd learn."

Home. "Many people have just arrived from ————

(another planet, a time machine, a sinking island, a disappearing country), and one of these people is going to live with each of our families. Tell as much as you can about what kind of person you would choose to live in your house."

Block. "People live in different places and surround themselves with different things for very different reasons. Where I live, for instance, is in some ways different from where you live, and in some ways the same. I like some of the things about where I live and don't like other things about it. From television, movies, magazines, we learn about how other people live. What are some of the things you would like to have happen in your neighborhood? What are some of the things and events in your neighborhood you'd miss if you moved?

Me. "Singers, movie actors, and athletes often have press agents. The press agent's job is to tell other people about the singer, actor, athlete—what he likes to do, his characteristics, who he likes to be with, his pet peeves, what his friends like about him, how his family is special, what he'd like to have happen in the future—all things his fans would like to know. Knowing most of this makes you like the actor or singer better. You're going to be your own agent. Tell me the kinds of things about you—as you are now— that you'd like to have other people know. If you exaggerate a little bit on anything, tell me."

"SPIES FROM XENON"

The children are told, "Pretend we are all people from another planet, Xenon, way out in space. We adults have sent you as spies down to Earth to find out what Earth kids are like. After a long visit you have come back. What do you have to tell us?" Each child is given four tickets. On one is printed the word "Mad"; on another, "Afraid"; on another, "Strong"; and on the fourth, "Happy." The kids go to each of four booths, using a ticket as before to tell the adults in the booths what they know about kids on Earth—

"What makes Earth kids mad? What makes them afraid?" The game ends when all kids have been to all booths.

Comments

The "spies" idea, at least as we used it, didn't seem to release the kids to tell us anything different from what we had heard in previous games. We all lost the "outer space" part of the game soon and were interviewing the kids about themselves. However, it is possible to use this technique to make children discuss feelings, if even at a superficial level. It surprised us that a ticket marked "Afraid," and a sign similarly marked, actually produced anything other than complete apathy or confusion for these kids. It worked in some sense. Some "spies" remarks are listed below as recorded at three of the booths.

At the "Mad" Booth
    When they're picked on or beaten up by kids, relatives, or teachers
    When friends are beat up
    When they're teased
    When they have to stay home and do chores
    When they fight with brothers, sisters, or friends
    When teachers are mean
    When somebody steals something
    When teachers make you do third-grade work [from a fourth-grader]

At the "Strong" Booth
    They lift weights and do exercise
    Eat their food
    Can pick up rocks and people and tall buildings
    When you play kickball and basketball
    A giant lady can pick up a lot

At the "Afraid" Booth
    Fights
    Fathers

Making a mistake and hurting someone
Getting hit with belt
Threatened by being hit with branch
Getting blamed for things they didn't do
Being hit with a razor strop
When he has to be in a play, make a speech
Night-time and when it's light

"MOOD MASKS"

Four adults move from one group to another (four groups). Each adult wears a paper-bag mask with a caption: "Mad," "Happy," "Sad," "Afraid." Each mask-wearer has an explanation for his mood as follows:

Mad—because the teacher gives me work that is too hard
Happy—because I won a fight with a bigger kid
Sad—because my best friend is going to move away
Afraid—because my mother might hit me with a strap

The children are told that their task is to guess why someone like them would be mad, happy, sad, or afraid. They can ask the rotating mask-wearers any "yes" or "no" questions. The people wearing the masks shift from group to group every 30 seconds. The team that has the most accurate information at the end of a time period is the winner.

VARIATION OF "MOOD MASKS"

The second time we played the game, all four mask-wearers (adults) had signs taped to their chests on which was printed the name of one of the adults (the same for all four). This time, the kids tried to guess why this person (whom they had known for a few weeks) would be feeling mad, happy, sad, or afraid. The kids guessed the adults were:

Mad—because the kids fight when the adult wants them to listen

Happy—because the kids like him

Sad—because he likes the kids, and he is not going to be with them much longer

Afraid—because he thinks the kids won't like today's games.

Comments

The game is a projective device. The children's guesses indicate something about why they think someone like them would feel a certain way. We didn't hear much that we hadn't heard before—mostly fights, beatings, monsters. The kids weren't as good at having ideas about "sad" and "afraid" as they were with "mad" and "happy." They were quite attentive and interested much of the time.

Their guesses about the person's feelings were much harder for them, particularly the sad and afraid ones. For those two feelings, they guessed mostly childish reasons: "Your mother left you alone." "Your friends think you're ugly." "A big lion might attack you in the night." Some had good adult-type guesses: "Your wife is fixing to leave you." "Your kids are sick."

When we had finished, we had the groups compare what they knew. Then they were told the "real" reasons for the person's feelings. A couple of the kids seemed interested, but mostly the reasons for "sad" and "afraid" didn't seem credible to them.

"AMNESIA"

When we arrived in the classroom, one of the staff members acted dazed and "out of it." We told the kids that he had been hit on the head and had lost his memory. We sat him down, put earphones on him, gave him a microphone, turned the tape recorder to "record," and suggested that they talk with him through the other microphone to help him remember what was going on and regain his memory. From time to time the amnesiac had questions for them.

Comments

The staff member is a good actor, and the kids were believers in his amnesia. A few remained skeptical for a long time, but they ended up convinced, we're pretty sure. They seemed a bit afraid, but only for a very short while, then were quite attentive and interested in his dilemma.

Most of the kids tried to get him to remember the names of other people in the group: "Who's that girl right there?" "Who's the boy who's always at the record player?" They quizzed him to see if he could remember the names of articles of clothing, of parts of his body, of the street he lived on, of the foods he liked for breakfast. Then they began to ask him about his family—was he married, did he have any brothers or sisters, did he have any children. One girl in particular tried terribly hard to teach him names of objects and to control the other kids so that he could learn "by himself."

Perhaps the most important use of the technique is to turn the kinds into teachers of an obviously inferior (temporarily) adult. It also allows the adult to ask difficult, crazy, offensive, personal, or embarrassing questions, because he needn't conform to the mores of remembering adults. Some questions the amnesiac might ask: "Why is your skin a different color than mine?" "Why are you so little?" "What am I doing here?" "What have I done to you in the past few days?" "Why do those kids fight all the time?" "Why do you all talk at once?"

"MIRROR"

The kids were told to "stand up in front of that mirror, look right at yourself, and say something nice to yourself." After each had said something (usually after encouragement or badgering by a staff member), he sat down. A period of their listening to their tape-recorded voices saying something nice to themselves at the mirror followed. Then (with the recorder turned on again) they were asked how it felt to hear their voices, and how it felt to do that with the mirror.

Comments

The exercise took on the qualities of a "test" situation, and the kids responded in some typical ways: Donna, a bright girl, had a temporary memory lapse; Mike, also bright, talked nervously and phonily; and a couple of girls just clammed up for most of the "conversation."

The mirror idea is worth pursuing. However, all of the children had a hard time saying something beyond "Hi," or "You're Brian," and their statements weren't surprising (I like you. I love you. You have a nice shirt. You're tall, you're pretty), except for one (Brian said, "Please come to me."). Some of the kids refused to come into the mirror booth.

Since these games were suggested to the project, many of them have been reformulated, restructured, and adapted for classroom use, with promising results. The original trials were meant to be suggestive, not conclusive. It should become increasingly obvious to the reader that the possibilities are boundless for inventing imaginative procedures by which children can begin to confront themselves, their feelings, and their concerns. We must now begin to involve ourselves more with the quality, effectiveness, and objectives of these procedures.

8

SOME REACTIONS TO A CURRICULUM OF AFFECT

Toward the close of the project, Gerald Weinstein interviewed a group of children who had participated in the Philadelphia Cooperative Schools Summer Program. The program drew its students from grades 4 to 12 in a cross section of Philadelphia schools, public, private, and parochial. It focused on an affective curriculum which was influenced by the model but was not a direct application of it.

The children appeared to be most appreciative of the innovative program, and many of their comments exemplified the kind of outcome the educators sought. We believe that it is fitting to give students the last word (to date) since it is toward responses from, and outcomes in, learners that the model is ultimately directed.

GW (*assuming the role of a cautious administrator*) : We're meeting in the Philadelphia school district building. I am in charge of making some changes in the Philadelphia schools. That's what this office is, the planning office. This is my staff and we've been principals in this system, and now we've been elevated to make decisions about principals and teachers. Somebody said we should see you because he thought you might have some suggestions about what we should be planning. Is that true? That you might have some suggestions and would you mind if we reacted to them? OK, would you present us with your case, then?

JANET: The only changes I can think of are so subtle and it's not something you would write down on paper—they're not changes in curriculum, they're changes in personality. After this summer, I think you could teach underwater basket weaving and have interested people if you just had the teachers to do it.

GW: Well, we've always said we needed good teachers, so you're really not saying anything new. You'll have to give us a little more to chew on.

STUDENT: Make school more interesting, not so boring. Broaden English to Communication, not just English, not just reading a book. Broaden it to really communicate.

GW: If you've had a chance to see our curriculum guide, you'll notice that all the Language Arts are under the title Communication.

STUDENT: Yeah, but they don't follow the same lines we were studying. They're not as broad. They're limited. For instance, you go to English class, you pick up a novel, you learn about that novel, but you never really relate it to what's outside, to what's real.

GW: Where did you learn more English? In your summer program or in our school?

STUDENT: Summer program.

GW: Wait a minute, does everybody agree with that?

STUDENT: It's different for everybody.

GW: Do you agree that you learned more English in your summer school than you did in regular school?

STUDENT: No. When we have school, the teachers are tough, and I guess we did learn more than we did in summer school. In regular school I learned more.

GW: You learned more.

STUDENT: I think I felt more in communication in the summer.

GW: Felt more? What differences does that make, that you felt more?

STUDENT: Well, that's the most important thing.

GW: You go to the movies and you feel, but that doesn't mean you learn anything. The job of the school is to teach you.

STUDENT: Yes, it does mean that you learn something. If you just go to English class and you don't feel anything, you just learn grammar all the time—you don't feel anything.

GW: Now wait a minute, in our curriculum guide there's more than grammar, there's literature.

HAROLD: Now the problem is that what the student gets is not necessarily what's in the guide. You can sit down and write guides all day until your fingers are numb and until the computer tape runs out, but that doesn't mean that what's on the paper gets to the students. I don't know, maybe that's because the teachers are so dry.

GW: Do you mean to tell me that schools have to be responsible for making you feel better?

HAROLD: I'm not saying necessarily to make you feel better, but to make you feel, period.

GW: You don't feel when you come to school?

HAROLD: I go to English class and sit there. In the summer school we read novels, and the teacher made comments about them, and he went into such depths of them that you go in on a depth of your own. You feel the novel, you feel like . . . for instance, we were reading part of *Damien the Leper*, and we had a discussion whether Damien the Leper or Madame Curie was supposed to be more motivated. This was more of a debate-type thing than where the teacher just puts down strict rules like, "Madame Curie gave more than Damien the Leper because she used a scientific method," or something like that. That's more of a debate. When you have these topics, I think you should throw them open to debate, not just plain discussion.

GW: What part do you think feeling has to do with learning in school?

JANET: Because people feel. You have to live with people, and people have feelings. They have emotions. You can't get around it, and in order to live with them, you have to learn about the emotions. You have to be able to understand them, and how can one understand them if you never learn about them, if you just sit and listen and never throw things open for debate, and they just teach it to you straight?

GW: So you'd like more debating?

STUDENT: Yeah, something that would bring out more emotion.

GW: It seems to me that what you people are saying is that if we had a school with a lot of emotional arguing going on, that this would be fine with you.

STUDENT: Yeah, it would.

JANET: You have to take an emotional argument with . . . well, for instance, this summer the big argument was freedom and how to learn to live with freedom, how to control it, to treat it, how to manipulate it, and I think that everybody learned that with freedom you have to take responsibility and it's the same kind of thing.

GW: There are a lot of things you don't know. Would you admit that? There are a lot of things you don't know that you have to be taught. Otherwise a lot of your feelings are not based on anything. So here you people are saying, "We want to come and feel and feel and argue," but a lot of times we have to teach you some knowledge on which to base your argument. So, I don't understand. When are you supposed to get the knowledge?

JANET: I think it's all based on how it's taught. The way I feel, you could have taken the same book that I had last year during English, and with that same book, in the summer program, I would have gotten twice as much out of it, *not because it was different material* because we used the same book.

GW: You mean you would have got more *feeling* out of it?

JANET: I'm not quite sure what they mean by feeling. I mean getting more out of them, more that I could argue. I can argue better because I read *Franny and Zooey* this summer than I could have from reading it by myself or with instruction at the school I go to, because it was discussed in a much different manner in the summer. It was discussed with the idea that we live in a world that is real, not that we live in the classroom of English and we're learning A, B, C, and D.

GW: Didn't you ever discuss a book in English class in regular school?

STUDENT: Yes.

GW: So, what's the point? You're not learning A, B, C, and D, are you?

JANET: Well, we don't discuss them the right way, that's what I'm saying. We discuss them like, "There are six minor characters. How do they affect the major characters," and so on.

GW: But when do you think you're supposed to learn how stories are made up and what the structure of literature is?

JANET: Yeah, but you can teach that, and you can teach it so much more painlessly.

GW: Did you learn the structure of literature, or were you busy arguing about the way the characters felt?

JANET: Yeah, I think we learned the structure as much as we learned anything . . . . And style—style is very important.

GW: OK. Tell me how you would have set up a debate in science on "Why Things Float."

HAROLD: Why couldn't you set up a debate on why things float? Of course you have so many theoretical arguments about why things float. You get one camp that can go over this way, another camp can go over that way.

GW: You mean to tell me that we should have debates on why things float or what magnetism is?

STUDENT: Man, what do *you* think? If people want to know what it is, have a debate. If people want to know why things float, let them debate about it, and then they'll find out.

STUDENT: The teachers in the summertime treated us more like people. They didn't just say, "OK, your name is John Williams, you sit in a chair. We're going to talk about science. An apple is an apple." And you say, "No," and they say, "An apple is an apple and I'm the teacher," and you had to shut up and accept it. In the summer program, whatever we felt, we were able to express it . . . express our thoughts without having the fear of the teacher saying, "Shut up."

GW: Oh sure, that's fine if you have all the time in the world, but the kids I talked to said they didn't learn as much in the summertime as they did in the winter.

JANET: I was just going to say that they don't know what learning is. If you asked some people they'd say, "Yeah, I learned more," because they think learning is a certain amount of chemistry formulas. I think I learned more. I couldn't put down on paper that I learned this, this, and this, but it made me a more confident person, a more whole person. That to me is learning. Maybe it's wrong, maybe I'm crazy, but that's what I felt when I came out, the feeling I got. The feeling was that I had got something, whereas I had been going to this school since fourth grade, and more and more and more, every year, I've felt there is nothing for me in this school. And yet six weeks of these people and I feel like I've learned something more than in all those ten years.

GW: Anybody else? How do you get emotion into science? It's very, very difficult.

HAROLD: Hold it. That's the whole problem today. People are just . . . I just finished reading a whole book on this. That's the whole problem today. People say, "Let's observe something, let's hypothesize about something, and that's cut and dried." But science is *filled* with emotion. One man who helped in the discovery of something got so emotional about it that he shot himself, killed himself. I mean, now maybe he was a nut, but science definitely does have emotion in it. You can't get emotion in science? Yes, you can. Einstein certainly had to be emotional.

GW: Not when he was collecting and interpreting the data. In fact, that was the whole scientific method, that you can't be emotional about your data.

HAROLD: You can't be emotional about your data? Oh, yes, you can too. Why do you think it's so necessary that theory and tests be checked and cross-checked? Because of the fact that two things interfere in scientific thought: one, bias; two, lack of randomness.

GW: OK, bias is based on emotion. Do you all feel the same way?

MELANIE: I agree about feeling because I know in school right now I feel so empty. It's not the same at all. When I was going through summer school, they'd throw out a question. All right, maybe I didn't say much about it, but I felt something toward it. I go to school now, and I'll sit in the classroom and they'll say, "We're going to read this short story. Now, could you tell me the author? Could you answer this question? Is it true or false? Could you tell me what this character means?" It's ridiculous. They don't do anything. They say, "Let's discuss it. Let's talk about it differently." They don't do it the way we did in the summer. I don't know what we should do. I don't think I know enough about myself, and I don't know enough about people to say what we should do, or how we can fix this problem that we have, but it is a problem, and I feel very empty.

GW: Here, now, in regular school, you feel empty? How many kids are as interested in emotion as you are? How typical do you think you are?

MELANIE: No one in our school is interested in it. . . . I sat in school today, and it was in geometry, and I sat, and I looked at everyone, and I said, "Now they're really not like I am at all," because I was so angry. She was teaching geometry. . . . It was nothing. She was saying that this plane is this plane, and that line runs that way, and I'm feeling awful, and I was looking at the people sitting there being their nice little selves . . . goody-goody girls sitting there, "Yes, Sister, you're right. I understand," and they didn't understand at all.

GW: Well, what was it that made you feel bad? That they were responding that way?

MELANIE: No, that they weren't being themselves. They weren't feeling anything.

GW: How do you know they weren't being themselves? Couldn't that have been themselves?

JANET: That could have been her six months ago.

GW: Could it? Was that you?

MELANIE: That was me.

GW: You mean that that experience you had this summer made you so different from them? And now you're unhappy?

MELANIE: I'm not unhappy.

GW: Well, you're uncomfortable.

MELANIE: I'm uncomfortable, but I'm not unhappy, because I think I'm more of a person. And, you know, I can accept myself.

GW: You're more uncomfortable, but you're not more unhappy. I don't understand.

JANET: It's not unhappy, it's just being aware of something. It makes you a little more unhappy, but at least it gives you a feeling of knowing why you have this frustrating feeling of sitting there thinking, "There must be something wrong with me because I don't like this. Everybody else likes this, and everybody else gets good marks, and why don't I?" That's the difference.

JACKIE: They have to agree with the teacher. If they don't, they'll get a big argument about it, like if you bring up something, and maybe you're right for a change, the teacher will say, like I had science this morning, and my teacher was talking about something, and I disagreed with him, and he had to take it to the book to prove that he was right . . . but, he was *wrong* and he still didn't apologize for hollering at me or anything. He just said, "See, you were right for once, well, take it for granted," and he just walked out of the classroom, and we were dismissed. But, over at the other school, when you're right or something, the teachers would say, "Yes, you were right. I'm sorry that I hollered at you," or something, and they'd apologize. They wouldn't holler, but they'd say, "I said I was right and I wasn't so I'm sorry," and they'd go on with the class.

STUDENT: If the teacher was a human being, no matter what the curriculum was, as long as they gave us an opportunity to be able to talk without giving so much direction, it'd be great. Also, if they'd leave it open for us to be able to have interchange with them, to be able to talk with them about something in class so that it's not all coming from the teacher, and it's not all right. The teacher should treat us like a human being.

STUDENT: They keep telling us in high school, a freshman is a quarter of a person, a sophomore is a half a person, and by the time you graduate you're four quarters of a person at last. *Then* you can have some respect. But we still have our *opinions*, and no one's opinion is wrong, because it's their own personal opinion.

GW: But, aren't you really learning what the real world is like? I mean, the real world is the kids in your classroom with you, they're reacting to a teacher in a way you say makes you very uncomfortable, but which do you think represents the real world, them or you? Isn't education supposed to prepare you for reality?

JANET: But, why can't you fight it? They won't let you fight. They won't let you change anything in school. They shovel it into you and don't let you do . . . change. It's not right.

GW: It's not right? That's not enough of an argument: "It's not right." Who said it's not? It that one of the commandments?

JANET: What is so good about society today that we should have to grow up and be like everybody else?

GW: Maybe you shouldn't have to, but that's what it is, and aren't schools supposed to prepare you for the society you're going to live in?

HAROLD: Based upon the old model, the school is supposed to prepare us for the society of today, but I think the school had better wake up, I mean, up to the fact that the *students* are here now and they're going to stay here from now until tomorrow, until another generation takes over. I think the main mistake of schools is teaching us from the old ways.

GW: Now, let me get something straight. I certainly agree with you that teachers are human beings, that you should be treated like human beings. At the same time—if I'm an industrial leader, and I have people I want to prepare for positions in my manufacturing firm, they have a lot of very important decisions to make that have to be cool, calm, collected, and rational and I don't want them *debating* about electrical circuits. They have to have certain technical skills to operate those machines, to program those machines and computers. If I allowed those emotional debates to go on in my factory, I'd go out of business in three hours.

STUDENT: But you wouldn't have those emotional debates in factories, probably because you'd have had them in school. You would already know.

GW: Then how is school getting you ready for my technical operation?

HAROLD: Now, what are you talking about, rational and controlled? I agree that every person on this earth, if possible, should be rational and controlled at times. But where do you get this business that school is supposed to teach us to be rational people, calm and collected people and copasetic people? I think if more people stood up in this world and stopped taking things on the basis of being so cut and dried, then this world would be a better place. I don't think you're talking about being cool, calm, and collected. I think you're talking about being cut and dried. In a case in question, specifically the Negro, what has been the philosophy from outside the ghetto for so many years? What has been the message into the ghetto?

GW: That they're second-class citizens.

STUDENT: No, let's be frank, that they're "dirty niggers." Now, some Negroes come out of the ghetto believing this. That's what they're told.

GW: But I don't think that's rational.

STUDENT: Everybody else thinks it's rational.

GW: I think they have to be very irrational if they're taking those messages as truth . . . about what the "nigger" is supposed to be.

HAROLD: Well, can't you transform that into school life? I'm not talking specifically about any one class or other, but can't you take that into school life? That what's necessarily irrational is conversely not what's so wrong? In other words, what's so irrational is not so wrong. If I jump up in the classroom and say, "Prof, you're wrong there," in your opinion would that be wrong?

GW: I'm a little confused as to how you're telling me this.

JANET: Take Harold's example of the ghetto and of the high school. In the ghetto, you're told certain things. When you get out of the ghetto, you believe them because you've been told them over and over again: "You're Negro, you're a second-class citizen." When you get into the high school, you're told certain things over and over again because you're not given this exchange, this respect.

GW: Are you given faulty information in the high school? You mean the high school is a reinforcement of the image that you're second-class citizens?

JANET: They reinforce any idea they want to. Every high school reinforces any idea it wants to. My high school reinforces the idea that we're all well-rounded, good girls who are going to grow up and go to Vassar and get married and that's it. That's the idea, when we come out of there—just like when you come out of the ghetto, you think you're second-class citizens—we come out thinking that we're first-rate citizens, and *that's* not necessarily true.

STUDENT: Or else you come out thinking, like they instill in you that you have to go to college to be a success, and being a success is making lots and lots of money. So maybe that isn't a success.

STUDENT: That's what we're being trained for in our school.

GW: You mean there are other ways of being a success?

STUDENT: Sure, of course . . . Good Lord!

GW: Without money? In this society? Come on, now,

you're really putting me on. You're telling me that money has nothing to do with success?

STUDENT: For your definition of success, obviously. But not for ours. Money isn't everything.

GW: You mean to tell me that you can find another route to success without making money? You don't have the need to make money? And you're going to do that?

STUDENT: Yes.

GW: Wait a minute, wait a minute. None of you is going to try to make money, now?

STUDENT: Well, that's ridiculous.

GW: What's ridiculous about it?

STUDENT: We want to eat.

GW: That's as far as it goes? In other words, you'd be satisfied with an income that just got you three square meals a day? (And that doesn't include pheasant under glass.)

STUDENT: So long as I was clean in my own opinion. So long as I kept my self-respect.

GW: But couldn't you make money and keep your self-respect?

STUDENT: Look, what we're saying is, you don't have to go to Harvard or Vassar to be a success in this world. Some of these people come out of high school well trained. Sure, they make money, but just because you make money doesn't automatically make you a success.

GW: First you say you don't like the message to certain people that they're not really as good as others, and then you don't like the messages that "You are good," like your's was, Janet.

JANET: I just don't like messages. I don't like to be steered in one specific direction, good, bad, or anywhere. I like to figure it out for myself. That's what we did this summer.

GW: From what age would you like to steer yourself? When did you figure you were ready to steer yourself? How old were you? Or did that just come from this summer?

JANET: No, it's been a long time.

HAROLD: I think you have to prepare people for steering themselves.

GW: And what prevented you from steering yourselves up to this point, if you really wanted to do it so badly?

HAROLD: Our teachers.

GW: You mean to tell me that if you really wanted to steer yourselves so badly, you'd let your teachers stop you?

HAROLD: Sure I let teachers stop me. What are you going to do about it? You can't defy teachers in school. But, possibly, before I get out of school, I'll get into trouble lots of times like I've always done before because, if a teacher is wrong, I'm going to tell him he's wrong.

GW: From now on, you're going to do that?

HAROLD: I've done it. I've done it before and I'll probably end up doing it again. If he's wrong, I'm going to tell him he's wrong. And if he wants to get into an argument about me, fine. If he wants to report me to the vice-principal I'll tell it to the vice-principal. If he wants to take it up to the highest court of the land, if he's going to make his own trouble like a fool, that's his problem. But if he's wrong, I'm going to tell him he's wrong. I figure that if a teacher isn't mature enough. . . .

GW: How do you know *you're* right?

HAROLD: I'm not going to stand up in class if I'm not sure about telling a teacher he's wrong, now. But, if it's based on fact or a teacher gives a flat opinion . . . .

GW: And opinion comes from feeling.

HAROLD: Hold it, let me finish my statement before we get into feeling. Suppose a teacher stands up in class, and he has a bunch of students that are liberal, except for one little schmo in the back there.

GW: I take it you don't allow people not to be liberal?

HAROLD: No, I mean you've got liberals and you've got conservatives. I'm just saying in this particular class, it happens to be liberals.

GW: Except for the one little "schmo."

STUDENT: And the teacher says, "Well, today we're going to discuss the war in Vietnam. Now, students, I'm sure you'll all agree that your country's policies of 'my country right or wrong,' and the Vietnam war are right." And the liberals jump up and say, "I disagree with you on that." In that case, it's merely opinion, and the teacher can argue with that student. But if the teacher is stupid enough to say to that student, "Now, look here, your opinion is wrong. You don't have an opinion. You're stupid!"—if that teacher is stupid enough and dumb enough to stand in that classroom, if he's not mature enough to accept the fact that there are other opinions in this world and he can be wrong, then I don't think he's a teacher. Maybe he is a second-, third-, fourth-rate, out-to-infinity teacher, but not a first-rate teacher.

GW: Let me explain, I've been role-playing with you.

STUDENTS: We know that. We got that all summer.

GW: You knew that all along?

STUDENTS: You're too intelligent a person to be that . . . . If you believed the things you said you wouldn't be here talking to us.

GW: Why not?

STUDENT: You'd have walked out by now probably.

GW: Let me ask you a straight question here. And this is a tough one. I know you've expressed it in other ways in some of the things you've written. But, I imagine for those of you who were there for the first time this summer, that when you went into the program, you talked to yourself in certain ways about yourself. Everybody does. Somehow, I got the impression that, as a result of your summer program, the way you were talking to yourself about yourself changed. Now, I don't know if that's true or not. But, if it is, I'd like to know what was the difference in your talk. I don't know if you can answer that.

JANET: I can. I talk to myself often. There's nobody else to talk to. . . . You sit there and you close your mind after a while. And you do the exact same thing to yourself and everybody around you that they're doing to you. They don't listen to your opinions, and then you don't listen to theirs. And that's just as bad, really.

GW: But what were you telling yourself about yourself?

JANET: A lot of the time I was telling myself that I was being a big, fat fool if I want to get ahead in this world. You've got to get good marks, you've got to go to college.

And I was resenting, resenting myself, resenting everything around me, and I was really unhappy about it. But then you get to the summer program, at least this is what happened to me. At first I was completely ignorant, I kept saying, sitting in those classes, "I'm not going to be able to contribute anything. I don't know anything about this. All these people have really been living in reality and I've been living in my little happy haven. I don't have anything to give here." And then I started realizing that I'm a person, and I have ideas and opinions, and they're worth as much as anybody else's, and I have more respect for myself.

GW: So, one of the messages to yourself was at the outset, "I really don't have much to contribute."

JANET: Yes, because for so long I just figured I must be a nobody because everybody else in my class got good marks, and I got just all-right marks.

GW: So, the marks were telling you something about yourself before the summer experience.

JANET: Yeah, and now I look at the marks and I say, "Who cares, I'm a happy person." I can get things out of it, and I can listen and try to separate the good from the bad and see what's worth hearing.

GW: I'd like to hear from each one of you on this, if possible.

STUDENT: Well, before the summer project, I'd built a wall around myself.

GW: Tell me what you were telling yourself in that wall.

STUDENT: I just kept telling myself that I wasn't any good and I didn't have anything to offer and I really was as stupid as everybody at school told me I was.

GW: How did they tell you you were stupid at school?

STUDENT: Well, marks, IQ tests, things like that.

GW: Did they give you the results of your IQ tests?

STUDENT: Never.

GW: Well, how can IQ tests . . . ?

STUDENT: Because, well, what they keep telling us, this is what's hard to understand, they keep saying at school if you get bad marks, "No, no you can do better. Your IQ tests say you can do better. Why aren't you doing better?

You're supposed to be doing better, and we know you're smarter than this." But really, underneath it, the teachers had no faith in me at all, in anything, I mean. If you try to start over again, it's impossible. Everything is based on your back record.

GW: And you believed them?

STUDENT: Of course I did, there was nothing else there for me to believe. What else did I have?

GW: Ok, then what happened?

STUDENT: Then I went to the summer project. And, of course, I'm not completely changed, but it's a little different, because I contributed things and gave ideas, and people accepted my ideas. People said, "Boy, you're really smart."

GW: So what do you tell yourself in regular school now?

STUDENT: Well, it's changed a little bit in that now I sort of accept the way I was in the past, and I keep telling myself, "I'm not going to let it get me down. I'm going to work hard and I'm going to try to change." I'm going to make my marks good, because I know that for *them* it's important, although it's not important for me. And in order to get what I want, I have to get good marks, and I have to go through the whole bit, the whole system.

GW: So, you're really doing better in your school work, now.

STUDENT: Well, I guess so. I can't really tell. But before I didn't care.

GW: So, you're conforming to the system more now?

STUDENT: Well, I'm conforming in one sense, I'm conforming in that I'm trying to get good marks, and I'm trying to go to college, and I'm trying to get the best education that they offer. But, I'm not conforming in that my main goal is that I'm going to fight the system in the end.

GW: But in order to do that you're going to buy the whole thing right now?

STUDENT: Not buy it, just do it.

HAROLD: Before the summer program, I set myself up on a pedestal, being all-knowing and all-wise and everything-I-say-goes-and-is-right, and all these other dumb people are just sitting around doing nothing.

GW: You really believed that?

HAROLD: Yeah, I did, to an extent, before the summer program. But getting other people's opinions of yourself can sometimes shake you up a little bit, and I admit that people's opinions at the summer program really shook me up.

GW: I really don't understand one thing so far. You say that up to this point you really felt you were great and you were on top of things, that mostly everybody else was on a lower stratum. And I imagine that you had heard a lot of opinions that weren't necessarily complimentary to you. Yet, in spite of it, you still maintained your superiority. Then, all of a sudden, you heard other opinions this summer, and that shook you up?

HAROLD: Now wait a minute, hold it. One specific instance. John Fitzgibbons, who is a conservative, myself being a liberal, got into an argument on Vietnam, and this is what really shook me. To make up for a lack of confidence in myself, I guess, I started to shout and really put him down. And I found out that by shouting and getting excited, I forgot the whole line of thought and the point. And I said something which was a complete surrender to his argument. I said, "Wait a minute now, you're Mister Superior. You can't do this." And all of a sudden, the idea struck me that maybe you're not right all the time. And I think some of the kids feel the same.

GW: So the changed message for you is what?

HAROLD: That other people have better opinions than mine, not necessarily better, but a right to their own opinions, and that mine is not necessarily the correct one for everybody else. Some are better than mine, some worse than mine. And I think the pedestal got blown up.

GW: How about you?

STUDENT: Well, it's just like what the others said. When you're in high school, if you're in a class, and you say something, and everybody don't agree, you know, you're set for a hard blow. You know, none of your friends agrees with you. Well, you're being told this for four straight years and you begin to . . . .

GW: By whom?

SOME REACTIONS TO A CURRICULUM OF AFFECT 209

STUDENT: By everybody, the kids in the class, the teacher, some of my best friends, and we've had debates, and I've given my opinion and was told I was wrong. And after four years I began to think, "Well, I must be wrong all the time." So I built a wall around myself, and I decided I wasn't going to make friends with nobody, and I was going to keep to myself, and so far I did, until the program started. And the first day in the program, the first thing I said to myself, "I wonder if anyone was like me. No, they probably ain't cause I know everybody in there must be of a higher level of intelligence than me, so I'll keep to myself." But, it seemed that everybody seemed to offer their help and said, "We can be friends." So, I decided to go along and join the rest of them.

GW: So, what do you tell yourself now?

STUDENT: I say to myself that if I have an opinion and everybody else don't agree with it, there's no need to give it up or drop it or anything. I say, "It can't be no good. Start over again. You can always have a second chance."

MELANIE: Mine wasn't exactly like theirs. Before, I listened to what the teachers said, and I said, "Yes, Sister, I agree with you." I was a little rebellious because I'd get fed up with it, and I would say what I had to say. And, I could stand on my own two feet, for a while. But, it was always as though I was giving in to them in the end. But, after the program, I think a lot of it helped me to know myself and to realize that there were different parts of me, that I had feelings inside of me that could be respected by other people, and that things I had to say were good, just for the simple fact that they were my own. Now I'll go to school, and I'll tell them, "I don't agree with you." I don't argue. I just get up and say, "I don't agree." I think that's good.

CATHY: Before the program, I thought I was different. It was like a secret. I thought I was a different type of girl. I was unique, you might say. But I didn't tell anyone. I thought, "Oh well, I'll grow old and die, and this is a secret that nobody will find out that Cathy was different." But if I were to give my opinion to my friends, they wouldn't agree with me. They'd look at me like I was strange or something, and then I'd say, "Oh well, never mind. Forget it."

And that would be the end of it, but I'd keep it up inside of me. And I used to think, the nuns kind of drummed it into me. They said, "You won't have an opinion before you're twenty-one. Then you can have opinions. Then you can be right. Before then, just keep your mouth closed because nothing you're going to say is going to be intelligent. Just wait till you're twenty-one." And I thought that you had to go to college, you had to do all that stuff, you know, and I think that if I hadn't gone to the summer program I would have fit into my academy very well. I'd be just like the rest of the girls, but I don't fit in there at all, I don't think.

GW: Isn't that harder for you?

CATHY: Well, in a way I feel that I've reached a point that these girls haven't reached yet. I feel that I know something that these girls don't know. They just haven't reached the point I've reached. I feel that I'm more mature than they are because I know myself a little better.

GW: What do you know?

CATHY: Well, I know more about the way I feel and why I feel the way I do, and these girls aren't even going to *wonder*. They don't want to find themselves, because the nuns want them to come out all alike. You're all going to be alike when you graduate.

HAROLD: I think one main problem is educators. You are educated. You're going to decide what the kids of tomorrow are going to have to learn. I just say this, "Don't stigmatize!" Just don't, because you're going to kill them. (I don't mean literally that you're going to shoot them down.)

GW: I don't know what the word "stigmatize" means.

HAROLD: All right, what I mean is drumming in their heads humdrum A plus B plus C. In other words, let them find out for themselves.

GW: Even though it may be a longer and harder process?

HAROLD: It'll be a harder process, but the kids will benefit more. And they'll learn more.

MRS. PLATTOR: What makes you so sure of that?

HAROLD: What makes me so sure of that? Because I've been through it.

MRS. PLATTOR: That doesn't tell me anything.

JANET: I know why I'm sure of that, because, for instance, I learned certain things at school that the teacher
would say, "Now here's what we're going to learn. You'll
learn it, and then you'll tell what you've learned." Then I'll
get out, and I'll be arguing with somebody about this point
I've learned in history, and I realize I know the facts but I
don't have the foggiest idea of what I'm talking about. I can
tell you all the dates, but I don't know why it's in my head. I
don't know why I think it, or how I ever reached those
conclusions because they really don't go with my ideas at all.
And then I went to the summer program, and now anything
that happened there I could argue with anyone, because I
know why I thought it, because I thought it out in the first
place by myself and I *felt* it. At the beginning of that program the whole faculty could have said, "You are going to
learn this, this, and this." And we would have learned it.
But, the way it happened, we learned the exact same things,
but we learned them through a longer process all by ourselves
and we knew why we'd learned them. And we came to the
exact same conclusions we would have if they'd told us, but
we did it by ourselves.

MRS. PLATTOR: I want to ask a question of "the pedestal"
over here, because he's the only one who, it seems to me,
might feel worse since the experience. In other words, he was
sort of put down during the summer, and yet he seems
to have thought that the summer was a valuable experience,
and I would think that he would feel worse, because now
he has a lesser opinion of himself than he did when he went
to the summer program. Can you explain why it doesn't
bother you?

HAROLD: I don't think I was more comfortable. I think I
was just fooling myself. I think I became more comfortable
after the summer program.

MRS. PLATTOR: What do you mean by that? How did you
become more comfortable?

HAROLD. Well, I didn't think I was on a pedestal.

MRS. PLATTOR: And that's more comfortable?

HAROLD: To me it's more comfortable. I don't know about
anybody else. I'm just saying that for me-the-person, it's

more comfortable to realize that I can make mistakes because before, if I made a mistake, I was sick. I really got sick. But now, if I make a mistake, that's life. It's only human.

GW: Suppose that you had the same climate that was there in the summer, the same climate that was there in the summer school, the same organization, the same teachers, the same relationships with teachers, the same teaching procedures, but you really were studying content you usually study in school. Would it have worked?

STUDENT: I think it would have worked for me because as I learned my lessons, I'd be learning more about myself. And that's interesting to me, you know? You have to live with yourself the rest of your life. I'd like to see it done.

GW: So you're really saying that it really doesn't make much difference what you study as long as you have that kind of a *situation* to study *in*, you would then make the same kind of progress.

. . .

TEACHER: Do you all feel that the opinions you have expressed are typical of the students of the summer school as being the student situation?

STUDENT: Yes. Everybody there would agree with this.

HAROLD: You know something. I want to be a scientist, but sometimes the scientific method makes me sick. You know, just the fact that it's so cold and hard.

GW: Well, you may decide to change. Be an accountant.

HAROLD: Maybe I'll become a teacher.

JANET: I feel completely different about the people around me because, well Harold said he feels more comfortable with people, a lot of people. I had stopped observing and stopped respecting and just considered them apart from me. I don't necessarily feel big buddy with everybody now. I'm not going to say I do, because I don't, but I feel they're people with their own opinions and really, I look at everybody as the fat lady, now. I know that sounds ridiculous, but everywhere I go, when I start to dislike somebody, I think, "The fat lady, the fat lady from *Franny and Zooey*." It's almost like a religion with me, I mean. I think of my teacher and realize that like the fat lady she's got problems of her own to contend with. She goes back to her home with nobody in it, really, and I start to realize, well, she's a person and not just a person who used to be out to kill me.

GW: And so you were able to answer the question, in what ways you were like the fat lady.

JANET: Yes, I talked to her, my teacher, just the other day, and I really sat there and started to understand a lot of why she was the way she was.

TEACHER: How much have you been able to socialize when you've gone back to your schools? I mean you and you, and you and you, you're in the same school. How much have you stuck with people who went to the summer school?

STUDENT: Hardly at all.

TEACHER: Not even for those of you in the same school now?

STUDENT: We just see each other in the hallways and say hello.

HAROLD: They go back to their own crowd.

TEACHER: Have you found any ways, any strategies almost, techniques . . . are you exerting any influence or change on your own old crowd? And if so, how?

STUDENT: Well, first of all, I never had an old crowd. Now the difference is that I'm talking to more people in my class. For instance, there's a girl in my class that I never really had a very high opinion of academically, and just the other day I was talking to her about the racial problem in Philadelphia and some of the things I've learned at the program. And I really talked to her and it's almost as though the same thing happened to this girl that has been happening to me all my life at my regular school, and she really is a smart girl. She really is intelligent, and she's got some really good ideas. And that's something I've learned about other people. I'm more open-minded.

HAROLD: I think in my school we have a group in there who are staunch. Well, they're so young, I don't think half of them know what they really think, I include myself, but they are left-wing liberals, and they look at everything from the point that only what is *not* the philosophy of "my country right or wrong" is right. And, in some ways, I've exerted an influence over these people trying to start—I don't say they've started yet—trying to look at their beliefs more realistically and look at the other man's beliefs as I had to do in the summer program. Now I say, "Well, look at what the other side has done, too, you know you've got to look at both sides." Before, I would have stuck in my own little clique. But the summer program opened my eyes to both sides of a problem. But, if I stayed on one side or the other, I couldn't do it. I think I have to keep myself, possibly, in the middle ground.

TEACHER: What happens to your home life? What is your relationship to your parents as a result of this summer? I'm asking because I think it's exceedingly important.

HAROLD: My mother's mad at me.

TEACHER: All your parents are angry at you?

HAROLD: My mother just says, she calls me "brother," "You know sometimes, brother, you honestly worry me." I can't debate with my mother on anything because, well, she's not that close-minded . . . .

TEACHER: She doesn't like you to debate with her?

HAROLD: No, she does, that's not the point. She wants me to disagree with her, but she wants her opinion to exert some influence. She's upset when her influence doesn't work, and consquently she and I are getting into many arguments. I think we're both richer for it, because I think she's beginning to think . . . .

GW: Well, what was it before?

HAROLD: I'd just shut up. Whenever she'd say, "Well, brother, I think you can put on a tie today and a white shirt today and go out and look nice." I'd put it on, and sometimes I'd disagree about which tie I'd want to put on . . . and now, different opinions about civil rights seem to come up.

GW: How about some of the others now?

JACKIE: Before, I used to regard my mother's opinion, but I'd fight back with her. She'd say something, and I'd say, "No, no," and we'd get in a big argument, and she'd always end up hollering at me. And my father would come downstairs and say to her, "Stop hollering at the kids." And my mother would shut up. Now it's my father who hollers at me. Now I tell them about the things I've learned in school and stuff, and I argue with him and everything because he doesn't know a thing and I don't know a thing. And now my mother tells him to be quiet, and he won't say anything, and then when she leaves, I'm back arguing again.

TEACHER: Why do you suppose that happened, Jackie? You're arguing with a different person. Why your father rather than your mother now? Did you ever stop to think about it? Are any of you having the same problem?

STUDENT: It's almost exactly the same thing. My mother will tell me now, "No, don't talk to me. You'll have to talk to your father." And I'll go talk to my father, and it's so different because, I don't know, my father will listen to my opinion. . . .

9
POSTSCRIPT

pproximately three years have elapsed since the first rough draft of this report was written. In retrospect it appears that our interests coincided with a national trend, a trend variously identified as the "human-potential movement," "personal growth," the "group movement," "sensitivity training," or, as a writer in *Nation* refers to it, "a rage for awareness." [1]

As a reaction to the purely rational, scientific, objective philosophies emphasizing the divisions between thought, feeling, and action, which have dominated our nation's institutions for so long, "the human potential movement," says

[1] D. Bess, *The Nation* (Feb. 20, 1967).

Newsweek, "is involving Americans in their biggest emotional binge since V.J. Day." [2] Encounter and training groups, says Carl Rogers, "are the most rapidly spreading social phenomenon in the country. They are helping break through the alienation and dehumanization of our culture." [3]

That the movement, whatever it is called, represents a popular (as opposed to a professional) development is demonstrated by the huge amount of publicity it has received in the mass media. Most large-circulation magazines have reported on some aspect of the trend within the last two years. *Life, Look,* and *Playboy* have published articles on everything from the Esalen Institute to guides for programs that are alternatives to psychoanalysis. *Psychology Today,* a new lay and professional magazine devoted to applied behavioral sciences has become a highly successful publishing venture, in part, we believe, because of the increasing public demand for more knowledge concerning "inner space." Hollywood, attuned to popular trends, has entered the arena with "Bob & Carol & Ted & Alice," a satirical treatment of a group encounter and its aftermath. *Joy,* by William Shutz, and George Leonard's *Education and Ecstasy* have both made the best-seller lists. And, finally, there are at least three new commercially produced parlor games dealing with sensitivity, therapy, and black-white relations.

This trend is beginning to find its way into the public schools under the labels "humanistic education," "affective education," and "psychological education." As Max Birnbaum has pointed out:

During the 1960's, public education discovered the emotions. Cognitive learning and skill training, the traditional components of education, no longer satisfied the needs of a generation that had experienced the civil rights revolt, the widening generation gap, the increasing confusion of teachers, administrators, and school board mem-

[2] "The Group: Joy on Thursday," *Newsweek* (May 12, 1969).
[3] "The Group Comes of Age," *Psychology Today* (Dec. 1969).

bers about ends and means in education. The result was a growing interest in various approaches to affective learning that assign to the emotional factor in education a role as important as—or perhaps, more important than—the traditional substantive content and skills.[4]

Alschuler reports,

At the frontier of psychology and education a new movement is emerging that attempts to promote psychological growth directly through educational courses. Psychologists are shifting their attention away from remedial help for the mentally ill to the goal of enhanced human potential in normal individuals. Educators, on the other hand, are beginning to accept these courses along with the unique content and pedagogy as appropriate for schools.[5]

It is, of course, encouraging to find ourselves forerunners of a significant trend. However, some specters are arising from the "faddishness" of the movement. Because of the easy accessibility of affective procedures and techniques, ethical issues, appropriateness, requisite competencies of teachers, and, above all, objectives of these procedures are being overlooked or ignored by novice educators. As a result, some children, parents, and community leaders have become disillusioned with the practice of using random affective techniques with children. "The pity is that this promising innovation may be killed before its unique properties have a fair chance to demonstrate their worth."[6]

What is needed is some discipline so that courses rather than techniques may be introduced in public education on a nationwide scale, courses that are soundly constructed, effec-

[4] "Sense About Sensitivity Training," *Saturday Review* (Nov. 15, 1969).

[5] Alfred Alschuler, "Psychological Education," *Journal for Humanistic Psychology* (Spring 1969).

[6] Birnbaum, *op. cit.*

tively taught, properly sequenced, and carefully evaluated.[7] At least 350 major approaches to dealing with psychological growth and some 3,000 affective exercises and techniques have been identified. But the affective-curriculum developer still needs some structures, models, or organizers that will help him to plan for specific outcomes—outcomes that can be clearly communicated to all concerned; that will help him to focus; that will help guide his selection of appropriate materials and procedures from the overwhelming number of alternatives that are now available. The model presented in this report is a beginning, a first small attempt at meeting this need.

[7] Within the last three years some responsible curriculum efforts have been initiated in this area. The greatest inroad in public schools has been in Philadelphia, under the enlightened leadership of Superintendent Mark Schedd and the creative efforts of Terry Borton, Norman Neuberg, and Henry Kopple. Experimental curricula dealing with pupils' affective concerns are now being used in many classrooms throughout the city. George Brown, in another Ford-sponsored project, has been setting up programs in California to train teachers in the use of affective approaches to instruction. A graduate program in Humanistic Education is now in operation at the University of Massachusetts. This program deals with curriculum development and teacher training in the areas of identity, connectedness, and power. In the New York State Department of Education at Albany, Alfred Alschuler is heading a program in research and development for psychological education and psychological educators. These are the programs with which we are most familiar; we have described only a few of the many responsible educational activities in this area. See T. Borton and N. Neuberg, "An Education for Student Concerns," Philadelphia Board of Education, Philadelphia, 1968; and G. Brown et al., "Now: The Human Dimension," A Ford Foundation Report, in press, 1970.

INDEX

New York State Department of Education, 220n
New York World's Fair of 1939–40, 152
Newsweek, 218
Nixon, Richard M., 8n
"Now: The Human Dimension" (report), 220n

"One-Way Glasses" strategy, 13, 67, 71–99; behavioral outcomes of, 76; and concerns and diagnosis, 73–76; content vehicles for, 78–93; evaluation of, 97–99; and learners, 72–73; and learning skills, 93–94; organizing ideas of, 77–78; teaching procedures used in, 94–96
Oral expression, 31
Organizing ideas, 46–50; definition of, 46–47; in identity education, 69, 77–78, 105
Otto, Herbert A., x, 91n, 133, 150

Parental influences on students, 103–4, 149–50
"Pathways" project, 99
Peace, concern for, 131
"Personal growth" movement, 217
Philadelphia Affective Education Project, 106
Philadelphia Cooperative Schools Summer Program, 163; affective techniques used in, 220n; students' reactions to curriculum of affect in, 193–216
Phillips, Lila J., ix, x
Phyllis and Terry (film), 132
Physical Science Study Committee (PSSC), 4, 20
Pilot projects, 6
Plattor, Emma and Stanton, x, 152
Playboy magazine, 218
Poetry, unit on, method of introducing, 26
Police, attitudes toward, 21–22
Pollution, 30
Poor, minority-group children: educational needs of, 4–5; failure-to-learn characteristic of,

8; and school's failure to teach, 17, 19; handicaps of, 4–5; improving education of, 3–4; learning styles of, 7n, 21, 56–58. *See also* Disadvantaged children
Potential of students, 32; achievement and, 27; "trumpet" and, 162
Potter, J. B., 40n
Power and powerlessness, students' concerns about, 29, 44; diagnosing clues to, 40–41, 133–51; and identity education, 73–75
Prelude (film), 106
Preschool education, 6
Private school groups: and "Faraway Island," 127–31; and "Ten Years from Now," 140–48
Problem solving, skill of, 53, 64
Process of Education, The (Bruner), 48n
Programmed instruction, 4, 30
Progressive education, 36
Promotions, grade, 26
"Psyching out" students, 123
Psychoanalysis, 218
Psychology, educational, 26
Psychology Today (magazine), 218
Puerto Ricans, 14

Racial prejudice of disadvantaged pupils, 5, 30
Racine (Wisconsin) public schools, 152–53
"Rage for awareness," 217
Rathbone, Charles, 149n
Readiness to learn, 8, 25
Reading, developing skill of, 25, 30, 31
Rein, Martin, 6n
Relevance of content, 10; affective as relevant content, 28–29; analysis of the nature of, 12; and causes of irrelevance, 21–22; and concerns of learners, 22; definition of, 23, 29; and learners' feelings, 21–22; need for, 19–23; and procedures not

"Them and Us" strategy, 67, 99–113; behavioral outcomes sought in, 104–5; concerns and diagnosis indicated in, 101–4; content vehicles used in, 105–10; evaluation of data of, 112–13; and learners, 100–101; and learning skills, 110–11; organizers used in, 105; teaching techniques used in, 111–12

Thought: abstract, 163, 165, 169–71; critical, 53; integration of, with concerns and action, 163–74

Tibbetts, John, x, 100

"Time Capsule" diagnostic technique, 122, 151–60; and East Orange Negro students, 153–54; evaluation of data of, 158–59; and New Orleans students, 154–57; and Racine students, 152–53; teaching procedures used in, 159–61

Time relationships, learner's, 9

Toward a Theory of Instruction (Bruner), 48n

"Trumpet," strategy, 162–74; abstractions used in, 163, 169–71; adaptation of, for use in Philadelphia program, 163; distinctions used in, 163 166–69; experimentation of, 163, 171–74; integration of person's concerns, thought, and action in, 162–65; inventory of feelings taken in, 163, 165–66; nature of, 162–63; process of integration in, 162–74; sequence of lessons in, 162–63

Tutorials, 4

University of Massachusetts, ix, 220

Upward Bound student group, Hoboken, New Jersey, 124–27, 129; and "Faraway Island," 123–29; and "Ten Years from Now," 134–40, 145–48

Value assumptions, questioning, 163, 169–71

Vietnam war, 159–60

Walters, Barbara, 123n

Weinstein, Gerald, ix, x, 13, 30n, 71, 123, 134, 193

Western Behavioral Sciences Institute (WBSI), 175

White middle-class norms, 14

White middle-class students, 20

"Who Am I?" experiment, 13

"Who Are You and Why Are You Special?" strategy, 67–71; behavioral outcomes sought in, 69; content vehicles used in, 69–71; and learners, 68; and learning skills, 71; organizers used in, 69; and students' concerns, 68–69; teaching procedures used in, 69–71